sweatshirt
remix

TRANSFORM ORDINARY
SWEATSHIRTS INTO
EXTRAORDINARY FASHIONS

Debra Quartermain

kp

CINCINNATI, OHIO
mycraftivity.com
connect. create. explore.

Published by Krause Publications, an imprint of F+W Media, Inc., 4700 East Galbraith Road, Cincinnati, Ohio, 45236. (800) 289-0963. First Edition.

Other fine Krause Publications titles are available from your local bookstore, craft supply store or online retailer; or visit our website at www.fwmedia.com.

13 12 11 10 09   5 4 3 2 1

DISTRIBUTED IN CANADA BY FRASER DIRECT
100 Armstrong Avenue
Georgetown, ON, Canada L7G 5S4
Tel: (905) 877-4411

**DISTRIBUTED IN THE U.K. AND EUROPE
BY DAVID & CHARLES**
Brunel House, Newton Abbot, Devon, TQ12 4PU, England
Tel: (+44) 1626 323200, Fax: (+44) 1626 323319
Email: postmaster@davidandcharles.co.uk

DISTRIBUTED IN AUSTRALIA BY CAPRICORN LINK
P.O. Box 704, S. Windsor NSW, 2756 Australia
Tel: (02) 4577-3555

Library of Congress Cataloging-in-Publication Data
Quartermain, Debra.
    Sweatshirt remix: transform ordinary sweatshirts into extraordinary fashions / Debra Quartermain.-- 1st ed.
        p. cm.
    Includes index.
    ISBN-13: 978-0-89689-645-1 (alk. paper)
1. Sweatshirts. 2. Sewing. I. Title.
    TT649.Q94 2009
    646'.3--dc22   2009001608

Edited by Nancy Breen
Designed by Julie Barnett
Production coordinated by Matt Wagner
Photography by Ric Deliantoni and Christine Polomsky
Illustrations & Artwork by Deborah Peyton
Pattern Illustrations by Charles Bliss Productions

Acknowledgments

Another book comes to life! I am so pleased to have the opportunity to share my love of creative sewing and fashion wearables. I am very grateful to have an audience who loves to sew, alter, embellish and develop their own unique style as much as I do.

Thank you to everyone involved, from acquisitions editor Candy Wiza, who gave me this opportunity for a sequel to my first book *Sweatshirts: Figure, Fit, Fashion*, to my editor Nancy Breen and designer Julie Barnett. Thank you to the models who make the designs look even better than I imagined. At home I am fortunate to work with good friend and talented illustrator Deborah Peyton, who created the delightful illustrations throughout the book and on the CD. Charles Bliss took my pattern pieces from ragged to polished.

Then there are the special people in my life who support and cheer me on, who overlook my endless enthusiasm for fabric and DIY shows. My daughters inspire me with their unique sense of style and confidence. Thank you for believing in me and my passion for my work.

Dedication

I dedicate this book to my mom, Elizabeth, who patiently and lovingly taught me to sew when I was a little girl. She gave me a wonderful gift: the love of needlearts and the beginning of my creative adventure.

contents

CD Index

Read Me

Projects
- *Patterns*
- *Materials Lists*
- *Cutting Plans*

Extras
- *Graphics*
- *Garment Labels*
- *Transfer Sheets*

introduction

Sewing for ourselves is rewarding and practical in several ways. Color, pattern and style are not dictated; rather, you have the choice to create a wearable that is uniquely yours.

Sweatshirts are simply constructed of a fabric that moves with the body and is very comfortable for the active lifestyles we lead. Whether you purchase your sweatshirt brand new, raid your closet or shop at a thrift store, you can transform an ordinary sweatshirt find into a stylish jacket or tunic.

Sweatshirts and Body Type

The basic sweatshirt is very functional but not attractive on every body type. I have the luxury of being tall, but I have wide hips and very narrow shoulders, so I drown in an ordinary sweatshirt. Still, I love the cozy comfort, especially in our wintry climate in New Brunswick, Canada!

This led me to want to do more than cut open the front of a sweatshirt and add an appliqué. I wanted to restructure the sweatshirt in different ways to make it more flattering to various body types without losing the comfort factor.

A sweatshirt with sloppy shoulders and a boxy shape, although not a good look, is a great piece for restyling. It provides an opportunity to give an article of clothing a second chance, whether you choose to style it as a cropped jacket or cozy loungewear. Even sweatshirts with too-long sleeves, stretched waistbands and outdated appliqués can be reclaimed.

With our different body types, clothing off the rack often does not fit quite right. You can use the techniques in this book on other kinds of garments as well.

Fashion Recycling

These days we are more conscious of the environment, our pocketbooks and being creatively unique. Recycling, reclaiming and remixing an item of clothing saves one more piece from the landfill. I styled many of the designs in this book so that a discarded out-of-date piece can be cut up and given a second chance to become a star in your wardrobe.

Today's sewer has a vast array of fabrics to choose from. Eco-friendly cottons and soy-based and bamboo lines have become readily available. Garments that cannot be saved can be cut up for their fabric and embellishments, an important part of reclaiming and remixing.

Transformation Techniques

Do you have other articles of clothing hanging around that are too good to throw out but you just don't wear anymore? These can be combined and transformed with techniques found in this book.

One whole chapter is devoted to reclaiming old sweatshirts and other garments to make an attractive new piece. However, *any* of the project designs work with a recycled sweatshirt.

Quickies

Short on time? Choose a quickie project design and transform a sweatshirt from *ho-hum* to *wow* in a couple hours.

Use the CD

The CD accompanying this book has extras to print out, like garment labels and graphic designs for appliqués, so you can make every project special. You can also print project materials lists to take with you as you shop for fabrics and trims.

Time to Create

If you love fashion and a fun creative challenge; if you want a wardrobe that makes a personal head-turning statement; if you love fabric and trims; and if you love to sew, you have picked the right book!

Get out your sewing machine, gather your tools and supplies, spread out your sweatshirts and fabrics—it's time to cut, sew and create fabulous fashions.

creative beginnings

The sewing journey begins here, with tips and advice to help you create all twenty altered and embellished sweatshirt designs in this book. From fabrics and sizing to embroidering special touches, everything is discussed.

Sweatshirt fabric lends itself to being cut, sewn and manipulated easily. Any size sweatshirt can be used for a project. Important features like the neckband vary little from one size or brand of sweatshirt to another. The shirt itself is the foundation to build upon.

Choose shaping details that are appropriate for your body type. Mix and match design elements you like from different chapters: A collar from one design will work well with another design as long as the neckline is cut in a similar way.

Cutting and construction techniques are thoroughly detailed in the steps to each project. On the CD that accompanies this book you'll find convenient full-size patterns and guides to print and use as well as graphics for appliqués and garment labels.

The projects in *Sweatshirt Remix* are easy, stylish, unique, fabulous *and* comfortable. Enjoy!

about the sweatshirt

What Size Is Your Shirt?

Run your shirt's measurements against those on this diagram to get a sense of how your sweatshirt compares to those used for projects in this book.

sweatshirt, you'll find a 5" (13 cm) difference in sweatshirt widths. Allowing for back and front, you would need an extra 10-12" (25-30cm) of the recommended fabric.

Most pattern pieces, like collars and cuffs, vary little whether you have a petite or plus-sized figure; neckbands and cuffs are similar from size to size. Much design styling is based on sweatshirts being any size.

Just remember to check all measurements before purchasing materials, and adjust for size differences—the width is especially important.

SWEATSHIRT BLEND

Sweatshirts are available in different blends.

A sweatshirt of 100 percent cotton works well with designs that use cotton fabrics. Cotton can shrink, so wash both the sweatshirt and the project fabrics before creating a garment.

Many cotton sweatshirts come prewashed with a vintage finish. These work well with cardigan-style designs. A blend, however, may work better for a dressy jacket.

A blend of 50 percent cotton and 50 percent man-made fibers like polyester combines the characteristics of cotton with polyester's ease of care. Polyester holds its shape and can be machine-washed and -dried without concerns about shrinkage. Other blends are available as well. Again, the one you choose is a matter of personal preference and sweatshirt style.

Regardless of the blend, sweatshirts are available in a rainbow of vibrant colors, making it even more fun to combine fabrics.

There are many brands and fiber blends of sweatshirts, and sizes vary from brand to brand. Some brands are designed with a more fitted shape and shoulder. Of course, traditional styling has a dropped shoulder and loose body shape for comfort; but by adding simple structure details at the shoulder or through the body, these sweatshirts can provide good fit as well as comfort. Choose a sweatshirt brand with a fit that you like.

The diagram above shows the sweatshirt measurements used for the projects in this book; these serve as a guideline. Each project's *Inspiration Board* also lists the size of sweatshirt used in the design, and the fabric amounts in the materials lists are based on that size. Before you buy materials for a project, measure the sweatshirt you plan to use and compare your measurements to the diagram. For example, if you are using a large sweatshirt to make a project based on a small

fabric

When shopping for fabric for a specific project, keep these things in mind:

· The design of the project you'll be making.

· The sweatshirt color and blend you'll be using.

· Whether the design calls for casual or dressy fabric.

· Any special design details.

Also, consider fabric types and how they perform. For instance, cottons work well with quilting details. Shop the fat quarters and remnants, as several of the project designs do not require large amounts of fabric.

Polar fleece is easy to sew in combination with sweatshirt material. There are many types and qualities of fleece available; choose a medium-weight fleece with a nonpill finish.

Flannel is a good alternative choice for bath or lounging robes such as those in Chapter Six: *Aaah, Spa Treats* (page 110).

A great option for discovering unique fabric is shopping for vintage garments. Unusual fabric pieces can be cut and used in a jacket, or the garment can be recycled into the sweatshirt design itself (see Chapter Five: *Recycled? Remarkable!*, page 88).

Fabulous Fabric

I have my own version of therapy: Fabric Therapy TM (Too Much), as in you can never have *too much* fabric. I'm fortunate to have friends in the industry that have supplied me with a blended array of fabric delights, such as Northcott and Loralie Designs™.

Different Sweatshirts, Different Blends

Individual blends can impact fit, shrinkage and ease of care.

trims

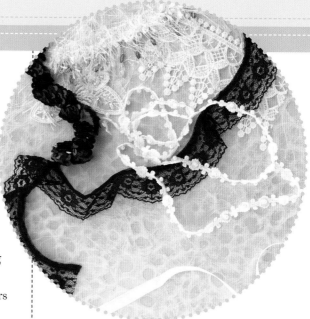

Trims and embellishments are just as important as fabric. Pick trims that not only match your garment but will stand up if the piece is washed frequently. For evening wear that may be professionally cleaned, durable trims and closures are less of a concern. If your trim is vintage or special in some way, the safest approach is to remove it before any type of cleaning.

Companies like Expo International offer an exciting collection of fringed and beaded braid. A wonderful array of specialty iron-on trims is available from makers such as Kreinik. Such trims make it quick and easy to create the look of embroidered detail on a jacket. Heat-set pearls, rhinestones and brads offer effective ways to embellish garments without a lot of hassle.

Through these details you can make a stylish and unique statement. You can also have great fun experimenting with a variety of beautiful trims.

BUTTONS AND THINGS

Buttons, clasps, toggles, snaps—there are so many to choose from. Remember the garment's design as you shop for buttons. Wood or heavy buttons work well for wool felt. For lighter fabrics, choose a more delicate button or closure.

I've suggested a variety of closures throughout the book for you to try. These add creative finishing details that make a garment stand out.

A Bounty of Beautiful Trims
From simple laces and ribbons to beaded eyelash fringe and sequined bands, the options for finding just the right trim for a project are abundant.

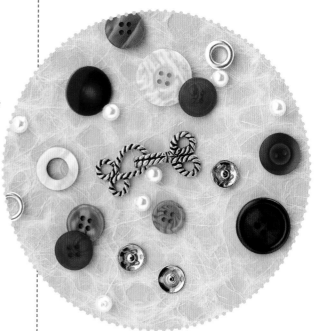

So Many to Choose From
Consider the design, the weight of the fabric and your personal style when selecting buttons and closures for a project.

tools

There are many tools and products that make the sewing experience easy and enjoyable. Below I've listed those that you'll find essential for making the projects in this book; many are basic tools you should have in your sewing area. See *Resources* on page 125 for shopping information.

THE ESSENTIALS

Make sure you have these tools close at hand whenever you begin a sweatshirt project.

Sewing Machine

For the designs in this book, a machine with a variety of stitches is best; the straight, zigzag and buttonhole stitches in particular are necessary.

However, you can make several of the designs in this book with just a simple straight stitch. If you are a novice sewer, choose a machine that isn't intimidating. The basic models all have several stitches that you can experiment with. As long as you can sew a straight line, you are good to go.

A serger comes in handy for finishing seams, but you can use a small zigzag stitch on a regular sewing machine instead. Machine embroidery can be used to further embellish many of the jackets.

Cutting Mat, Rotary Cutter and Wide Ruler

These are indispensable for cutting fabrics and straightening sweatshirt edges. Shop for quality tools by makers such as Fiskars.

Scissors

It's best to have scissors in different sizes. Note that you'll need sharp pointed scissors for doing reverse appliqué.

A Few Basic Tools
Clockwise from upper left: embroidery hoop, pins and pincushion, cutting mat, rotary cutter, ruler, chalk, scissors, mini iron and heat-set applicator.

Iron and Mini Iron

Pressing at every step of a project's creation ensures the best results, so keep your iron handy. In addition, a mini iron is perfect for smoothing small details and pressing seams. It can also affix iron-on threads.

Pins

I prefer long quilter's pins with colored heads. They're easy to pull in and out, and the contrasting colors show up well against fabrics.

Needles

Sewing machine needles that work well with fleece are a universal size 70 or 80 needle; for handwork, use an embroidery, or crewel, needle size 3–9.

Quilter's Pencil and/or Chalk

These are used to draw pattern lines and mark details for cutting and sewing.

Embroidery Hoop

For hand embroidery, a hoop is necessary to hold the fabric taut while stitching.

Transfer Paper

Also known as dressmaker's carbon, this product is great for transferring designs for hand embroidery and appliqué.

Iron-On Adhesive

Fusible products (including interfacing and quilt batting) are excellent for fusing fabrics and stabilizing hems. Interfacing and lightweight quilt batting give body to collars and cuffs. Try brands like HeatnBond for adhesives in tape and sheets as well as iron-on interfacing and fleece.

Add Images to Your Garments
Images and graphics can be printed to iron-on transfer sheets or special fabric sheets made especially for printers. You'll find selected graphics on the CD that accompanies this book.

SPECIAL TOOLS

These tools are for adding unique finishing details for extra flair or making it easier to work on (and enjoy making) your project.

Heat-Set Applicator

With this tool you can easily affix crystals, rhinestones and studs, which are available with adhesive preapplied. The tip holds the embellishment and heats the glue; you simply press the embellishment into place. There are a variety of makers of heat-set applicators and embellishments, such as Kandi Corp.

Multiuse Textile Tools

Multiuse textile tools offer interchangeable tips, which makes them versatile and suited to a number of tasks. For instance, Walnut Hollow's Creative Textile Tool™ comes with seven unique tips for pressing seams, fusing fabrics, cutting stencils, embossing velvet and more.

High-Definition Task Lighting

Lamps that provide ultraspectrum or natural lighting for detailed work, such as those made by OttLite®, ease eye strain and allow you to see accurately the colors you're working with.

Sweatshirt Cutting Basics

Each project includes detailed step-by-step sweatshirt cutting instructions as well as an *Inspiration Board* that illustrates the cuts to be made for that project. However, here is a demonstration of the basic approach to cutting a sweatshirt, with additional details you'll be glad to know.

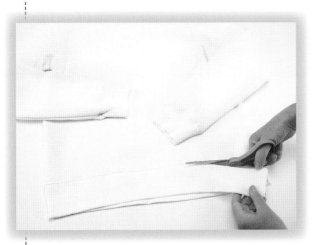

1 Remove the bottom band and the cuffs from the sweatshirt by cutting close to the stitching lines. The neckband can be removed in the same manner, but many of the designs keep this as a collar.

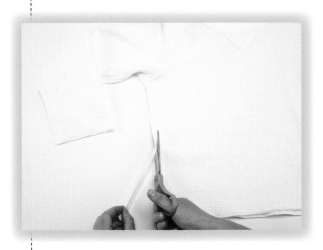

2 Turn the sweatshirt inside out. Cut carefully along the side seams close to the stitch line. If the sweatshirt does not have side seams, draw a line from the underarm down the side of the sweatshirt and cut along this line.

This step makes it easier to work on the garment because you can lay it out completely flat.

Stitching Lines = Staystitching

The stitching line on a sweatshirt can act as staystitching when left intact. This is suitable for certain designs and a time-saver as well.

Tips for Sweatshirt Design Success

• **Staystitch ¼" (6mm) around all edges** unless otherwise instructed to help stabilize the sweatshirt shape. Some designs also leave the stitching at the neck, shoulders and bottom band for stabilizing (see *Stitching Lines=Staystitching* above).

• **Press thoroughly at every step.** Pressing is important because it gives a polished appearance to the finished wearable, especially when designs have pleated elements.

• **Double-check the design measurements** against the sweatshirt you are using for the project before you sew a single stitch.

• **Print out any pattern pieces** required from the CD that accompanies this book. Tape pattern segments together to create larger patterns where indicated. Some pattern pieces will need to be flipped on the center line in order to cut a complete fabric piece.

3 Lay the sweatshirt flat. Use a rotary cutter, cutting mat and quilting ruler to straighten edges and to trim specified measurements from the bottom of the sweatshirt according to individual project instructions.

4 Measure and cut the front center of the sweatshirt using a rotary cutter and ruler.

From this point, other cut variations in projects can be made easily according to individual instructions and pattern pieces.

5 For vests, measure and cut sleeves 1" (25mm) beyond the shoulder seam line.

For ¾ sleeves, cut off the arms of the sweatshirt according to individual project measurements using a rotary cutter, cutting mat and ruler.

Some Sewing Terms: A Quick Guide

Seams: Sew 2 separate pieces of fabric right sides together with a ½" (13mm) width sewing line (or seam allowance) unless otherwise indicated.

Finish seams: After sewing seams, trim to ¼" (6mm); serge the raw edges or use a small zigzag stitch to finish.

Staystitching: Before sewing the garment, stitch inside the seam allowance to stabilize the stretch of the sweatshirt. Usually done on a single thickness at ¼" (6mm) width.

Topstitching: Sew a ¼"-wide (6mm) line of stitching that shows on the right side of the fabric; can be decorative or functional.

adding embroidery

Embroidery is a beautiful way to add a unique touch to a sweatshirt design. Here are a few basic stitches that are adaptable to many uses; the diagram on this page also shows some decorative embroidery stitches to try.

In addition, *Doing Embroidered Appliqué* on page 23 demonstrates how to combine embroidery with a simple appliqué technique using iron-on adhesive.

STRAIGHT STITCH

Simply bring the needle up through the fabric, then insert it back through the fabric at the end of a straight line. Repeat as needed.

BACKSTITCH

Bring the needle up through the fabric, then insert the needle one stitch length behind the first hole and pull through. Bring the needle up through the fabric a stitch length ahead of the first hole, then insert the needle through the first hole, pulling the thread through. Each stitch goes *back* through the front hole of the previous stitch.

RUNNING STITCH

Bring the needle up through the fabric, then take it back down one stitch length ahead. Bring the needle back up through the fabric a stitch length ahead of the previous stitch. The stitch line should resemble a dashed line, with stitches and spaces of an even length.

FRENCH KNOT

Bring the needle up through the fabric, then wrap the thread twice around the needle. (The thread should be snug but not so tight that the needle won't slide through.) Keep the wrapped thread in place on the needle and insert the needle into the fabric, pulling needle and thread through the wrapped thread to close the knot.

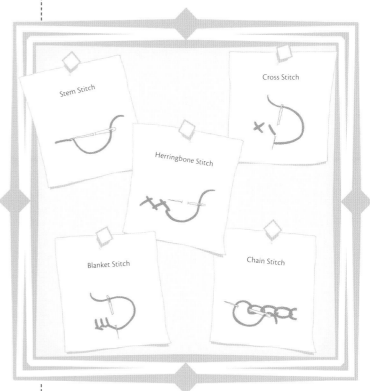

Embroidery Stitches
There are a variety of basic embroidery stitches that can be used with appliqué or to enhance elements of a sweatshirt design. Detailed instructions for these stitches are available in most embroidery books and online.

ooh la la chic!

Styled with flair, these trendy short tunics and jackets combine vibrant colors, embellished details and comfort fit for must-have additions to any wardrobe.

Today's popular pairing of a short jacket with a longer blouse or lace camisole is nothing new. The short jacket was first worn by women near the end of the seventeenth century, although men had been wearing it for centuries, first as a short overcoat with tails. The story goes that the Earl of Spencer was warming himself with his back to the fire when he got a little too close. The tails of his jacket caught fire, so he cut them off—and the short jacket was born. It was adapted to women's fashion to be worn with the long dress styles of the day.

The short jacket works with every body type, and a collar frames our real beauty and most important facial features: the eyes and smile. This style can be worn by anyone, and the look can be changed significantly depending on what other pieces are chosen.

Create a signature look with your favorite color combination and put a new outfit together in an evening. Design details are easily applied for a boutique-quality finish. Adding a polished tunic or jacket is the quickest way to complete a put-together look.

YOU WILL NEED

1 navy sweatshirt

1 white sweatshirt

½ yd. (46cm) silk floral fabric

One 9" × 12" (23cm × 30cm) piece light teal wool felt

One 9" × 12" (23cm × 30cm) piece dark teal wool felt

1 yd. (91cm) narrow elastic

¼ yd. (23cm) iron-on adhesive (fusible web)

1 package pink heat-set crystals

1 package heat-set pearl studs

1 skein white embroidery floss or pearl cotton

1 skein lilac embroidery floss or pearl cotton

Cutting mat

Embroidery needle

Heat-set applicator

Iron and board

Large ruler

Matching and contrasting thread

Quilt pencil or chalk (white)

Pins

Rotary cutter

Scissors

Sewing machine

Classy Bouquet Tunic

The classic combination of navy and white, along with the attractive detailing of a bouquet of silk watercolor yo-yo flowers showcases this feminine blouse-style tunic. The textured wool felt embroidered leaves are a striking contrast to the soft silk, adding design dimension. The ruffled sleeve with edged border completes the sophisticated contrast.

Finished length: 25" (64cm).

Fit and Style

This tunic-style blouse with detailed neckline and relaxed fit brings attention to the face and flatters a thicker waistline by skimming over it without extra bulk.

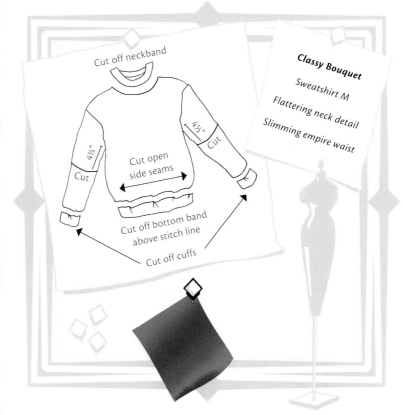

Inspiration Board for *Classy Bouquet Tunic*
See the size and measurement guide on page 8 and compare the measurements of the sweatshirt you're using.

Back View of
Classy Bouquet Tunic

PATTERNS TO PRINT FROM CD:

Curve guide (Sheet #0-A01)

Leaf and large circle templates (Sheet #0-D01)

CUTTING PLAN

Cut the bottom band from the white sweatshirt for the neckband.

Cut the bottom band from the navy sweatshirt for the belt.

Cut two 4" × 30" (10cm × 76cm) bottom ruffle pieces from the white sweatshirt.

Cut two 9" × 20" (23cm × 51cm) sleeve ruffle pieces from the white sweatshirt.

Cut two 3" × 22" (8cm × 56cm) sleeve trim pieces from the silk.

Cut one 3" × 32" (8cm × 81cm) belt trim piece from the silk.

Cut nine 6" (15cm) yo-yo flower circles from the silk.

Cut 4 leaves* from each piece of wool felt.

Apply fusible web to the wool felt before cutting out the leaves (follow manufacturer's instructions).

Cut the Sweatshirt

1 Refer to the *Inspiration Board* on page 19 for the project cutting diagram. Cut the bottom band from the white sweatshirt as well as the sleeve and bottom ruffle pieces.

2 Cut the bottom band from the navy sweatshirt above the stitch line; also cut off the cuffs and the neckband. Cut the sweatshirt open along the side seams.

3 Measure down the sleeves 4½" (11cm) from the underarm seams. Cut the sleeves off along this line.

4 With the sweatshirt front folded in half, place the curve guide along the edge, matching dots, and mark a line with quilt pencil or chalk. Cut along this line.

5 Cut two 4" × 20" (10cm × 51cm) cuff pieces from the cutoff sleeves.

TIP: If the sleeve is not wide enough to cut 2 pieces 4" × 20" (10cm × 51cm), cut 4 pieces 4" × 10½" (10cm × 27cm), then sew the 2 pieces together.

Sew the Tunic Pieces

1 With the white bottom band piece folded with wrong sides together, sew a ½" (13mm) casing along the folded edge.

2 Measure the white band piece along the cut neck edge to check for fit. Stretch slightly to fit if needed.

3 Leave ⅜" (9mm) extra for the seam allowance at the end before pinning. Begin at the center back or shoulder seam of the sweatshirt and pin the open end of the white band to the neck edge. Leave ⅜" (9mm) at the opposite end.

4 Sew the band to the neck edge.

5 Sew a ⅜" (9mm) back seam, leaving the casing open; finish the edges.

Sew the Sleeves

1 Sew 2 rows of gathering stitches ¼" (6mm) apart along the top of each white sleeve piece.

2 Press the navy in half lengthwise with wrong sides together.

3 Press under ½" (13mm) on each long side of the silk sleeve pieces.

4 Center the silk strip on the front side of the navy cuff piece. Gather every 4" (10cm) and pin.

5 Use 6 strands of lilac embroidery floss or 1 strand of lilac pearl cotton to stitch the silk trim into place at each pin.

TIP: The floss or pearl cotton won't show on the inside of the cuff if you take the needle through the cuff's upper layer only. Tie off each stitch. Repeat for the remainder of the strip and for the second cuff.

6 With the cuff folded wrong sides together, pin it to the bottom of the sleeve ruffle. Sew the cuff and sleeve ruffle together and press.
   Repeat for the second cuff.

7 Pull the stitches at the top of the white sleeve piece to fit the ends of the navy sweatshirt sleeve. Pin in place. Sew the sleeve; finish and press.

Sew the Bottom Ruffle

1 Press a ¾" (19mm) hem along the long sides of the bottom ruffle. Topstitch 2 rows ¼" (6mm) apart along this edge.

2 Sew 2 rows of gathering stitches ¼" (6mm) apart along the opposite long sides of the ruffle.

3 Pull the gathering stitches of both pieces to fit the bottom of the navy sweatshirt, 1 for the front and 1 for the back. Pin in place.

4 Sew the ruffles. Before finishing, double-check that the front and back line up. Press and finish the seams.

Sew the Side Seams

1 Fold the sweatshirt with right sides together along the side seam. Align all the seams of the sleeves and ruffles.

2 At the center point of the seam line, measure 1" (25mm) in and mark.

3 From this point draw a line gradually narrowing to ½" (13mm) at either end of the seam.

4 Sew along this line. Finish and press.

TIP: A curving side seam is figure-flattering and eliminates a boxy look.

About Yo-Yos

Yo-yos are created from fabric circles of varying sizes, usually 3–6" (8–15cm) in diameter. Buttons or beads can be added to the yo-yo center, or yo-yos of different sizes can be stacked for a rosette effect.

Make the Embroidered Bouquet

1 Press ¼" (6mm) around the edge of each 6" (15cm) floral silk circle.

2 Sew around the edge of each circle. Pull the threads tight and secure.

3 Press each yo-yo with the gathers centered. For a softer look, finger press the flowers instead of using an iron.

4 With a heat-set applicator, affix 3 pink crystals to the sewn center of each yo-yo flower.

5 Cut out leaves according to the *Cutting Plan* on page 19. Following the photo above and on page 1823,, arrange the leaves and flowers. Iron to fuse the leaves in place.

6 Before continuing, see *Doing Embroidered Appliqué* on page 23 and *Adding Embroidery* on page 15 for technique and stitch directions.

7 Use 6 strands of white embroidery floss or 1 strand of white pearl cotton to stitch the leaves with a straight stitch.

8 Use 6 strands of lilac embroidery floss or 1 strand of lilac pearl cotton to embroider the vines.

9 Sew the yo-yo flowers into place through their centers to the neckline of the tunic.

10 With the heat-set applicator, apply pearl studs in groups of 3 between the vines.

Practice on Scraps

Before applying heat-set embellishments to the actual garment, experiment on scrap pieces of sweatshirt fabric to ensure you obtain the desired results.

DOING EMBROIDERED APPLIQUÉ

Working with a simple leaf shape, here's how to fuse an appliqué piece with iron-on adhesive and enhance it with embroidery. An embroidery hoop can stabilize the sweatshirt while stitching the appliqué. See *Adding Embroidery* on page 15 for a brief primer on the stitches used.

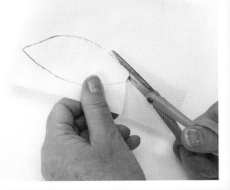

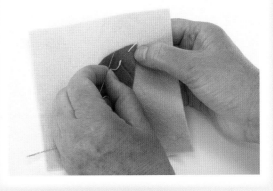

1 Cutting Out the Leaf
Apply iron-on adhesive to the leaf fabric according to manufacturer's instructions. Draw a leaf shape on the paper backing of the adhesive and cut out the leaf. Peel off the paper backing and iron to fuse the leaf to the background fabric.

2 Backstitching the Vein Down the Center of the Leaf
Thread a needle with 6 strands of embroidery floss or a single strand of pearl cotton knotted at one end. Bring the needle up through the fabric just in front of the leaf tip. Make the first stitch so it catches the leaf tip. Backstitch a vein down the center of the leaf.

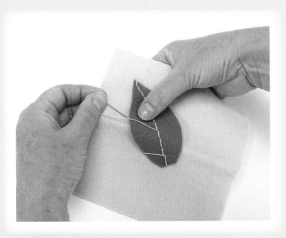

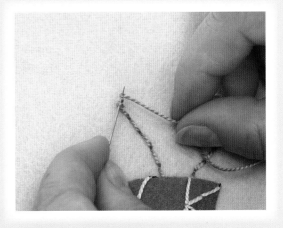

3 Embroider Veins with Straight Stitches
Embroider straight stitches from the vein to the outer edge of the leave, working up one side and coming down the other.

4 Creating a French Knot
With a contrasting color of floss or pearl cotton, backstitch vines around the leaf. Embellish the end of each vine with a French knot.

Sew the Belt

1 Turn the navy bottom band inside out. Turn each end in ½" (13mm) and press. Slipstitch the ends shut.

2 Press under ½" (13mm) on each long side of the silk belt trim piece. Pin to the belt and gather every 4" (10cm).

3 Use 6 strands of lilac floss or a single length of lilac pearl cotton and 1 stitch to hold the silk in place at each pin.

4 Sew a yo-yo flower to each end of the belt.

Add the Finishing Touches

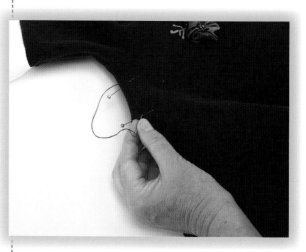

1 With matching thread, sew the belt loops on the side seams ½" (13mm) below the underarm seam. Insert the belt to be tied at the front or the back.

2 Use a safety pin to thread the elastic through the neck casing. Try the tunic top on to determine how tight the elastic should be.

3 Cut the elastic and sew the ends together. Slide them into the seam and finish off.

YOU WILL NEED

1 dark pink sweatshirt

½ yd. (46cm) floral fabric

1 yd. (91cm) polka-dot taffeta

Two 1" (25mm) buttons

2 snaps

1"-wide (25mm) metal ruler

Cutting mat

Iron and board

Large ruler

Matching and contrasting thread

Needle

Pins

Quilt pencil or chalk (white)

Rotary cutter

Scissors

Sewing machine

Polka-Dot Style Jacket

Polka-dot taffeta punches up this showy side-wrap jacket with its detailed knife pleats and diagonal tuck seaming. The shimmery fabric finish is highlighted in contrast with the solid depths of the sweatshirt fleece.

Remnant shopping can turn up wonderful fabric selections to combine into a gorgeous garment. Colorful button accents complete this jazzy jacket.

Finished length: 22" (56cm).

Fit and Style

A side-wrapped jacket with a high waistline slims the figure, and the short pleated bottom balances the figure. For a different look, lengthen the pleated bottom to the hip line.

Inspiration Board for *Polka-Dot Style Jacket*

See the size and measurement guide on page 8 and compare the measurements of the sweatshirt you're using.

Back View of
Polka-Dot Style Jacket

PATTERNS TO BE PRINTED FROM CD:

None

CUTTING PLAN

Cut one 5" × 45" (13cm × 114cm) neck/front trim piece from floral fabric.

Cut one 3" × 45" (8cm × 114cm) neck/front trim piece from polka-dot taffeta.

Cut two 6" × 25" (15cm × 64cm) waistband pieces from floral fabric.

Cut three 8" × 45" (20cm × 114cm) bottom pieces from polka-dot taffeta.

Cut two 6" × 14" (15cm × 36cm) sleeve trim pieces from floral fabric.

Cut two 3" × 14" (8cm × 36cm) sleeve trim pieces from polka-dot taffeta.

Cut one 9" × 10" × 13" (23cm × 25cm × 33cm) triangle piece from cutoff bottom of sweatshirt.

Cut the Sweatshirt

1 Refer to the *Inspiration Board* on page 26 for the project cutting diagram. Cut the neckband from the sweatshirt, leaving the stitching for reinforcement; cut off the bottom band and cuffs.

2 Cut the sweatshirt open along the side seams.

3 Measure down 6" (15cm) from the underarm. Cut the sweatshirt front and back along this line.

4 Measure and cut 6" (15cm) off each sleeve length.

5 Draw a line from the right front neck edge at the shoulder to the lower front bottom of the sweatshirt.

6 Along that line, measure 6" (15cm) from the shoulder and make a mark. Draw a line from this mark to the opposite shoulder. Cut along both lines.

7 On the excess bottom sweatshirt piece, draw a right angle with measurements of 9" (23cm) and 10" (25cm) for the triangle piece. Draw a third line joining the ends of the right triangle.

8 Cut the triangle piece carefully along the chalk lines.

Sew the Sweatshirt Tucks

1 With right sides together, align the sweatshirt triangle piece with the lower edge of the left-hand side of the jacket. This will create underlap for the jacket.

2 Use the angle of the cut front to begin drawing tuck lines 1¼" (32mm) apart. Draw from the edge to the shoulder.

3 Overlap the jacket fronts and continue drawing tuck lines to the opposite shoulder.

4 Fold along each tuck line 1 at a time. Sew ⅛" (3mm) tucks.

5 Measure and draw 5 straight tuck lines 1¼" (32mm) apart on the center back. Sew ⅛" (3mm) tucks.

Sew the Polka-Dot Jacket Neck/Front and Sleeve Trim

1 Fold and press under ½" (13mm) on either long side of the polka-dot fabric. Fold with wrong sides together and press in half again.

2 Pin the polka-dot fabric, sandwiching the raw sweat-shirt neck and front edge between finished trim layers, and topstitch into place.

3 Repeat steps 1 and 2 for the sleeve ends with 14" (36cm) pieces of polka-dot fabric.

Sew the Floral Jacket Neck/Front and Sleeve Trim

1 Fold the floral trim piece in half lengthwise, right sides together, and sew on all 3 sides, leaving a small center opening to turn.

2 Clip corners, turn and press.

3 With the seam side in, pin within the edge of the polka-dot jacket trim. Topstitch along that same stitch line.

4 Repeat steps 1 and 2 for the sleeve ends with 14" (36cm) pieces of floral fabric.

5 Pin the sleeve trim pieces into place, leaving ¾" (19mm) extending beyond the sweatshirt seam edges, and topstitch.

6 Line up the sleeve and side seams. Sew, finish and press.

Make the Pleated Jacket Bottom

1 Sew the polka-dot pieces together end-to-end to create 1 jacket bottom piece.

2 For the hem, press ½" (13mm) under on 1 long side of the bottom piece, then press ¾" (19mm) under and topstitch.

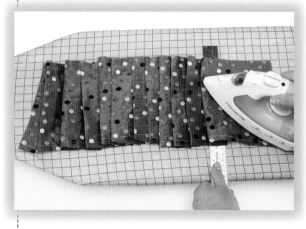

3 Use a 1" (25mm) metal ruler to create knife pleats 1" (25mm) wide and 1½" (38mm) apart. Press and pin the pleats to hold in place.

4 Sew across the top of the pleated piece ½" (13mm) from the edge to secure the pleats. Remove the pins.

5 Position the end of the pleated piece 2½" (6cm) from the inside jacket edge. Measure the bottom of the sweatshirt and compare to the length measurement of the pleated piece. Add 1" (25mm) to the sweatshirt bottom measurement for finishing the ends of the pleated piece. Trim off any excess beyond this measurement from the pleated piece.

6 Press the opposite ends of the pleated piece under ¼" (6mm) and repeat. Topstitch the ends.

7 Beginning 2½" (6cm) from the inside right jacket flap, pin the pleated bottom piece to the lower outer edge of the jacket. Sew the pleated bottom piece into place.

Sew the Jacket Waistband

1 With right sides together, match and sew 2 short ends of the jacket waistband pieces. Fold the waistband in half, right sides together. Sew on all sides, leaving a small center opening for turning.

2 Clip the corners and press. Turn right side out.

3 Center the waistband on the front side of the jacket along the upper edge of the pleat line; pin into place. Topstitch the waistband into place on all 4 sides.

Finish the Jacket

1 Sew 2 buttons to the right side of the front end of the waistband.

2 Sew 2 snaps on the wrong side of the front end of the waistband.

3 Overlap the jacket, aligning the snaps where they should meet on the right side of the bottom end of the waistband. When you've determined placement, stitch the snaps to the bottom end.

1 teal sweatshirt

2 striped linen tea towels

One 9" × 18" (23cm × 46cm) piece brown wool felt

3" (8cm) length ¼"-wide (6mm) elastic

¼ yd. (23cm) iron-on interfacing

¼ yd. (23cm) iron-on adhesive

1 roll iron-on adhesive tape

1" (25mm) brown button

1 package each pearl heat-set studs (white and gold)*

1 skein white embroidery floss or pearl cotton

Cutting mat

Heat-set applicator

Iron and board

Large ruler

Matching thread

Needle

Pins

Quilt pencil or chalk (white)

Rotary cutter

Scissors

Sewing machine

*I used Kandi Corp studs

Daisy Crop Jacket

Fashion can be expensive, but style doesn't have to be! A couple of department store linen tea towels are transformed into a clever collar and trim to compliment this eye-catching cropped jacket. A simple embroidered daisy design in rich wool felt accents the front. Heat-set pearl studs complete the piece with tasteful embellishment.

Finished length: 18" (46cm).

Fit and Style

This smart cropped jacket is just right over a blouse and dress pants for a comfortable, professional daytime outfit. The short style works well for petites and compliments a wider waist area by skimming it with a straight garment line.

Inspiration Board for *Daisy Crop Jacket*
See the size and measurement guide on page 8 and compare the measurements of the sweatshirt you're using.

Back View of
Daisy Crop Jacket

PATTERNS TO BE PRINTED FROM CD:

Collar piece 1 and small daisy petal template (Sheet #2-C01)

Collar piece 2 and large daisy petal template (Sheet #2-C02)

CUTTING PLAN

Cut 4 collar pieces from tea towels.

Cut 2 collar pieces from interfacing.

Cut two 3" × 18" (8cm × 46cm) jacket trim pieces from tea towel.

Cut 5 small daisy petals* from wool felt.

Cut 5 large daisy petals* from wool felt.

*Apply iron-on adhesive to the wool before cutting (follow manufacturer's instructions).

Cut the Sweatshirt

1 Refer to the *Inspiration Board* on page 31 for the project cutting diagram. Cut the cuffs and bottom band from the sweatshirt, leaving the neckband for a closer fitting collar.

2 Measure and cut 3" (8cm) off the bottom of the sweatshirt and 6" (15cm) off the ends of the sleeves.

3 Fold and press the sweatshirt, then cut open along the center front line.

Finish the Hems

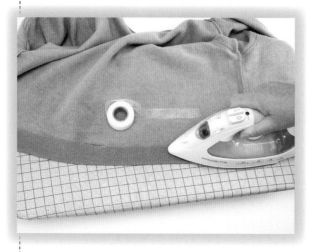

1 Press a 1½" (38mm) hem along the jacket bottom and a 1¼" (32mm) hem on both sleeves.

2 Adhere the hems with iron-on tape following manufacturer's instructions.

Sew the Front Trim

1 Press the front trim pieces in half, then press ½" (13mm) under along 1 long side of each piece. This will be the finished inside edge of the jacket.

2 Topstitch ¼" (6mm) in from the folded long side on both pieces.

3 Measure the hemmed jacket front. Use that measurement to press under the excess top and bottom ends of the trim pieces.

4 Align the right sides of the jacket front edge with the raw edge of the trim pieces and sew. Fold the trim over to the inside edge of the jacket. Use iron-on tape to fuse the trim into place.

Sew the Collar

1 Apply interfacing to the wrong side of 2 collar pieces.

2 Match the collar pieces in pairs with right sides together and sew all the way around, leaving a small center opening for turning as marked on the pattern.

3 Clip the curves and corners, then turn and press the 2 collar pieces.

4 Pin the right side of 1 collar piece to the wrong side of the neckband beginning at the front trim edge. Repeat for the second collar piece on the opposite front edge. The collar pieces will overlap ½" (13mm) at the the back.

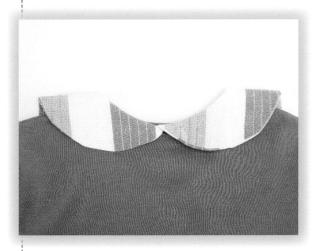

5 Sew the collar to the band and press.

Embroider the Daisies

1 Measure 2" (5cm) up from the hem of the right jacket front. Refer to the photo on page 30 for placement and fuse the large daisy petals to the jacket front.

2 Outline stitch around the edge of each petal with floss or pearl cotton (the pearl studs are applied later).

3 With the white quilt pencil or chalk, draw an 8" (20cm) curved stem as shown in the photo. Use floss or pearl cotton to backstitch the stem line.

4 Measure 3½" (9cm) from the left shoulder. Refer to the photo on page 30 for placement and fuse the small daisy petals to jacket.

5 Repeat steps 2–3 for embroidering the petals and creating the daisy stem.

Affix the Pearl Studs

1. With the heat-set applicator, apply 5 white pearl studs to the center line of each small daisy petal.

2. Apply 6 white pearl studs evenly spaced to the center line of each large daisy petal.

3. Apply 3 gold pearl studs spaced 2" (5cm) apart along each of the embroidered stem lines (see step 1 photo for placement).

4. Along the edge of each sleeve, space 5 double-row groupings of 3 pearl studs, alternating gold and white. Groupings should be 2" (5cm) apart, with 1" (25mm) between the double rows.
   When spaced, affix the pearl studs with the heat-set applicator.

5. Space 3 rows of gold pearl studs along the curve of each collar front and affix.

Add the Button Closure

1. Sew the button to the top edge of the jacket front trim just under the collar.

2. Make a loop from elastic and pull over the button. Adjust the loop size to fit the button snugly.

3. Sew the loop to the opposite side of the jacket front under the collar.

YOU WILL NEED

1 burgundy sweatshirt

½ yd. (46cm) embroidered fabric

2 large snaps

¼ yd. (23cm) iron-on interfacing

2¼ yds. (2m) white beaded trim

Four 1" (25mm) white buttons

Cutting mat

Iron and board

Large ruler

Matching and contrasting thread

Needle

Pins

Quilt pencil or chalk (white)

Rotary cutter

Scissors

Sewing machine

Ruby Babe! Jacket

Fluffy white beaded trim and rich embroidered velvet accentuate this dressy little jacket.

There are many beautiful embroidered fabrics to choose from, or embroider your own fabric with a custom design. Choose a fabric from the velvet family for elegant results. A tabbed front closure very easily adds a flattering double-breasted effect.

Finished length: 21" (53cm).

Fit and Style

This rich velvet jacket with contrasting detail is dressy enough for an evening out when paired with dark jeans and gorgeous boots. Add a silky camisole underneath or a soft thin knit for the always-popular layered look.

Cut open

Cut open

Cut

Cut

Cut off cuffs

Cut off bottom band

Cut off cuffs

Cut open side seams

Cut open side seams

Ruby Babe!

Sweatshirt M

Slightly fitted to give slimming middle silhouette

Inspiration Board for *Ruby Babe! Jacket*

See the size and measurement guide on page 8 and compare the measurements of the sweatshirt you're using.

**Back View of
*Ruby Babe! Jacket***

PATTERNS TO PRINT FROM CD:

Curve guide (Sheet #0-A01)

Collar pattern pieces 1 and 2 (Sheets #0-C01 and #0-C02)

CUTTING PLAN

Cut 2 collar pieces from the embroidered fabric.

Cut 1 collar piece from the iron-on interfacing.

Cut two 9" × 11" (23cm × 28cm) cuffs from the embroidered fabric.

Cut two 3" × 6" (8cm × 15cm) front tab pieces from the embroidered fabric.

Cut the Sweatshirt

1 Refer to *Inspiration Board* on page 36 for the project cutting diagram. Cut the cuffs and bottom band from the sweatshirt, leaving the neckband for a closer fitting collar.

2 Cut the sweatshirt open along the side seams.

3 Fold the sweatshirt in half and press, then cut open along the center front line.

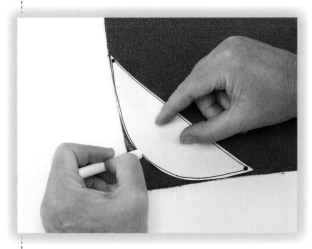

4 Place the curve pattern guide along 1 lower front edge of the sweatshirt, matching the dots on the guide to the edge of the sweatshirt. Mark the curve and cut carefully along the line. Repeat for the opposite lower front edge, making sure the curves line up.

Fitting the Shoulder with Pleats

This technique narrows the shoulder. It can be used on a larger sweatshirt to fit the shoulder while the rest of the sweatshirt remains roomy for a looser style jacket. The pleating also adds decorative detailing to the finished design.

Depending on the shoulder width, the pleat size can vary from 1–2" (25–51mm) and 2–4 pleats total.

The pleat width depends on the size of the sweatshirt and its shoulder drop. Try a sweatshirt on inside out and pin a couple of pleats to see what size pleat works best.

Sew the Shoulder Pleats

1 Lay the sweatshirt flat, wrong side up.

2 Beginning at the shoulder seam, measure 1–2" (25–51mm) and mark. Repeat twice more.

3 Measure 3" (8cm) on either side of the shoulder seam (6"[15cm] in total pleat length). Draw lines along these marks. Repeat for the other shoulder.

4 Press along the drawn pleat lines, then sew ¼" (6mm) on 1 side of each pleat line.

5 Press in 1 direction toward the shoulder.

Sew the Cuffs

1 Fold the cuff pieces in half lengthwise with right sides together.

2 Sew the ends of both cuffs, leaving the long side open on each. Trim, turn and press.

3 Sew 2 rows of gathering stitches ¼" (6mm) apart along the sleeve ends.

4 Pull the stitches to fit the cuffs, leaving ½" (13mm) for the seam on either side of the sleeve ends.

5 With right sides together, sew the cuffs to the sleeve ends. Press.

Sew the Collar

1 Apply interfacing to the wrong side of 1 collar piece.

2 Match the collar pieces with right sides together and sew on all sides, leaving a small center opening as shown on the pattern.

3 Clip curves and corners. Turn and press the collar.

4 Pin the collar to the top edge of the neckband ½" (13mm) from the edge with the right side of the collar against the inside edge of the neckband. The collar will stand up nicely when flipped to the outside.

5 Sew the collar into place.

Apply the Trim

1 Sew and finish the side seams.

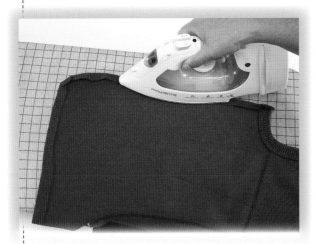

2 Press the edge of the sweatshirt ½" (13mm) to the right side, all the way around from opposite sides of the front to the back.

3 Pin the trim beginning under the collar at the front and continue completely around the jacket. Sew the trim into place. **Note:** This technique gives a nice finished edge to the jacket as the raw edge is covered by trim.

Sew the Tabs

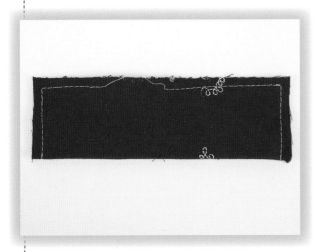

1 Fold the 2 tab pieces in half with right sides together. Sew along 3 sides of each, leaving a 2" (5cm) opening to turn. Clip the corners, turn the tabs and press. Topstitch the tabs.

2 Place the jacket flat with the front sides aligned.

3 Measure down 3½" (9cm) from the collar edge for placement of the first tab; center on right and left jacket fronts and pin into place.

4 Measure 3" (8cm) from the first tab and pin the second tab into place.

5 Unpin the left sides of both tabs but leave the pins in place on the jacket to mark snap placement.

6 Sew a button to the end of the pinned right side of each of the 2 tabs, stitching through to the wrong side of the jacket.

7 Sew 2 buttons to the right side of each of the left tab ends and sew snap tops to the wrong side of the tabs. Sew snap bottoms to the jacket at the pins.

clever quickies

Short on time but want big style? The projects in this chapter are designed to be easy and fast—ready to wear in two to three hours. Even ten or fifteen minutes here and there devoted to a project quickly add up to a finished piece.

Appliqués take the plainest of sweatshirts to an eye-catching level. Simply cut out a motif, iron on and add threads. Have some fun, let trim wander and swirl across the garment. Vertical or asymmetrical lines are visually interesting.

Iron-on appliqués are a quick way to add personality to a sweatshirt. The CD that accompanies this book contains graphics that can be printed on transfer sheets or printable fabric, allowing you to personalize a sweatshirt quickly and show off your sewing passion.

There are many iron-on embellishments available in sewing and craft stores and online that instantly add dynamic detail to a plain-jane sweatshirt. Be sure to follow the manufacturer's instructions for the best results.

Check the remnant bins at fabric stores for great deals on leftover bits and pieces.

The projects in this chapter can be picked up and put down as you have time. Bag and label them as you work so it will be easy to pick up where you left off.

In this chapter, time-saving techniques deliver dynamite designs for definite fashion must-haves!

YOU WILL NEED

1 white sweatshirt

1 yd. (91cm) polyester or lightweight knit fabric with a graphic print

1 yd. (91cm) narrow elastic

2 yds. (1.8m) 1"-wide (25mm) black satin ribbon

3½ yds. (3.2m) ½"-wide (13mm) rhinestone trim

Cutting mat

Iron and board

Large ruler

Matching and contrasting thread

Needle

Pins

Quilt pencil or chalk (white)

Rotary cutter

Scissors

Sewing machine

Bold Contrast Blouse

This striking black-and-white blouse with an empire waist combines a fabulous print fabric remnant and rhinestone trim with a sweatshirt bodice. The result is a flattering feminine top that's easy to make.

This project is ideal for a sweatshirt that has stains or worn spots.

Finished length: 21" (53cm).

Fit and Style

This style can be worn by most body types. If you prefer a longer look, just buy more fabric and extend the length or add a long lacy camisole underneath.

Inspiration Board for *Bold Contrast Blouse*

See the size and measurement guide on page 8 and compare the measurements of the sweatshirt you're using.

Back View of
Bold Contrast Blouse

PATTERNS TO BE PRINTED FROM CD:

None

CUTTING PLAN

Cut two 12" × 24" (30cm × 61cm) bottom pieces from print fabric.

Cut two 18" × 20" (46cm × 51cm) sleeve pieces from print fabric.

Cut one 6" × 8" (15cm × 20cm) neck insert piece from print fabric.

Cut one 48" (122cm) bottom piece from trim.

Cut two 18" (46cm) sleeve pieces from trim.

Cut the Sweatshirt

1 Refer to the *Inspiration Board* on page 43 for the project cutting diagram. Cut the bottom band, neckband and cuffs from the sweatshirt.

2 Cut the sweatshirt open along the side seams. Measure 5" (13cm) down from the underarm seams and cut off the sweatshirt at this line, front and back.

3 Carefully cut the sleeves off just below the stitching line (the stitching line acts as staystitching around the sleeve opening).

4 Measure the center point of the sweatshirt front at the bottom edge. Draw a line from each shoulder to the center point and cut along these lines.

Make the Sleeves

1 Lay 2 fabric sleeve pieces flat with right sides together.

2 Using the removed sweatshirt sleeve as a pattern piece, lay it flat on top of the fabric sleeve pieces, aligning the top of the sweatshirt sleeve with the top edges of the sleeve fabric.

3 Add 1" (25mm) to each end of the shoulder curve of the sweatshirt sleeve and mark on the top layer of the matched fabric pieces. From that point on each side, draw a line on the fabric that angles outward to create a sleeve with a total width of 18" (46cm).

4 Trace around the curved top of the sweatshirt sleeve. Cut the sleeves from both layers of fabric along all the drawn lines.

5 Sew 2 rows of gathering stitches ¼" (6mm) apart along the curved top of each sleeve.

6 For the hems, press the end of each sleeve ½" (13mm) under and then 1" (25mm) again. Topstitch into place.

7 With right sides together, pin the top of each sleeve to the armhole opening, pulling the gathering stitches to ease the fit.

8 Sew the sleeves, clipping the curves. Hand-stitch trim across the bottom of each sleeve 2" (5cm) from the edge.

Finish the Neckline

1. Measure the neckline. Cut the ribbon 1" (25mm) longer than the neckline measurement and press the ribbon in half lengthwise with wrong sides together.

2. Beginning at the front edge of the sweatshirt, fold the ribbon over the raw edge of the neckline and sew into place.

3. Hand-stitch rhinestone trim over top of the ribbon.

Sew the Top

1. On each side of the sweatshirt, align the sleeves and underarms. Pin and sew, beginning at the sleeve hems. Clip the curves.

2. Press the lower edge of the sweatshirt under 1" (25mm).

3. Sew the 2 fabric bottom pieces together, matching the ends. Press 1 long side of the fabric bottom piece under ½" (13mm), then again 1" (25mm) for the hem. Topstitch into place.

4. On the opposite long side of the bottom piece, press 1" (25mm) to the right side for the casing.

5. Hand-stitch trim 3" (8cm) from the hemmed edge of the bottom piece.

6. Pin the right side of the fabric bottom piece to the wrong side of the sweatshirt top, matching up the pressed 1" (25mm) casing folds. If necessary, stretch the sweatshirt to make it fit the bottom fabric piece.

7. Topstitch along either edge of the fold to create the casing.

8. Cut 2 pieces of ribbon each 12" (30cm) in length.

9. Measure under the rib cage and add 1" (25mm). Cut a piece of elastic to this measurement.

10. Sew the ribbon ends to the elastic. Insert 1 ribbon end into the casing and pull through to the opposite end.

Finish the Neck Insert

1. Press and sew a ¼" (6mm) hem on all 4 sides of the neck insert.

2. Pin the insert inside the neck edge. Try on the blouse. Adjust the seam line, if needed, to lie flat.

3. Sew the insert into the neck edge along the neckline.

YOU WILL NEED

1 pink sweatshirt

1 blue sweatshirt

1 package 3mm heat-set rhinestone mix

1 package each 5mm heat-set rhinestones (pink, blue, purple)

1 skein each embroidery floss or 1 ball each pearl cotton (green, lilac, yellow)

1 spool each #16 iron-on braid (yellow, lime green, blue, pink)

Cutting mat

Embroidery needle

Iron and board

Heat-set applicator

Large ruler

Matching and contrasting thread

Mini iron

Needle

Pins

Quilt pencil or chalk (white)

Rotary cutter

Scissors

Sewing machine

Double Fun Bolero Jacket

Two sweatshirts are combined in this cozy, reversible bolero jacket punctuated with trendy metallic braids and bling courtesy of heat-set sparkly rhinestones. The pocket adds detailing and a perfect place for an iPod or cell phone—stay connected and look good, thanks to one young-at-heart jacket.

Finished length: 19" (48cm).

Fit and Style

This is a great little jacket for traveling since reversible styling gives two looks for one. Make it black and white for a dramatic version. Add a matching camisole by swirling braid in a random design all over and heat-set rhinestones along the neckline.

*For blue sweatshirt; cut 5" from pink sweatshirt sleeves

Cut open

Cut

Cut

Cut

Cut

Cut

3"

3"

3"

3"

Cut off cuffs

Cut off cuffs

Cut off cuffs

Cut off bottom band

Double Fun

Sweatshirt S

Lengthens a short frame

Inspiration Board for *Double Fun Bolero Jacket*

See the size and measurement guide on page 8 and compare the measurements of the sweatshirt you're using.

Back View of
Double Fun Bolero Jacket

PATTERNS TO BE PRINTED FROM CD:

Curve guide (Sheet #0-A01)

Pocket (Sheet #3-A01)

CUTTING PLAN

Cut 2 pocket pieces from cutoff discards of blue sweatshirt.

Cut three 8" (20cm) lengths of each color of braid for the jacket spirals.

Cut one 12" (30cm) length of each color of braid for the pocket spiral.

Cut the Sweatshirts

1 Refer to the *Inspiration Board* on page 47 for the project cutting diagram. Cut the bottom band and cuffs from both sweatshirts.

2 Measure and cut 3" (8cm) from the bottom of each sweatshirt; 3" (8cm) from the blue sweatshirt sleeves; and 5" (13cm) from the pink sweatshirt sleeves.

3 Cut 1 pocket from the bottom discarded piece of blue sweatshirt.

A Second Pocket

Cut another pocket in pink and add it to the reverse of the jacket if desired. Embellish the reverse pocket or leave plain.

4 Mark the center front line on both sweatshirts and cut them open.

5 Line up the curve guide at the lower front edges of both sweatshirts. Draw curves and cut both sweatshirt fronts.

Sew the Pocket

1 Sew the pocket pieces with right sides together, leaving a small opening to turn.

2 Turn and press the pocket.

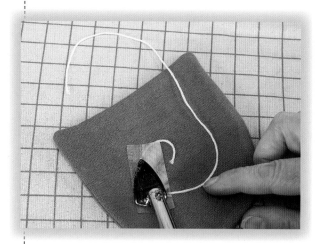

3 Arrange the 12" (30cm) yellow braid piece to form the inside of the swirl on the pocket; iron into place. Repeat with the lime green braid, then end with the pink braid as the outside of the swirl.

4 Heat-set three 5mm rhinestones (1 of each color) to the center of the swirl and 3 assorted 3mm rhinestones as shown in the photo on page 46.

5 On the right side of the pink reverse of the jacket, position the pocket 3½" (9cm) from the side and 3" (8cm) from the bottom. Pin the pocket into place.

6 Using 6 strands of green floss or 1 strand of green pearl cotton, blanket stitch the pocket to the sweatshirt. (Refer to Chapter One, page 15 for a stitching diagram.)

Sew the Sweatshirts

1 Place the sweatshirts with right sides together, aligning all raw edges, and pin. Sew the sweatshirts together
leaving the neck open. Clip the curves and turn.

2 Insert the blue sleeves into the pink sleeves with
wrong sides together. Press 2" (5cm) of the blue sleeve
to the right side of the pink sleeve to form a cuff. Topstitch
into place.

3 Pin the neckbands together.

4 Blanket stitch the entire edge of the jacket with
6 strands of lilac floss or 1 strand of lilac pearl cotton.

5 Fold the upper right corner of the jacket opening
2" (5cm) from the neckband and press so the blue
reverse of the lapel shows.

6 Repeat for the left lapel.

Apply the Swirls

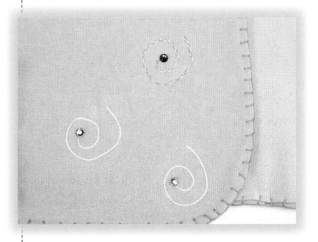

1 Using the above photo and the photo on page 46 as a
reference, arrange 3 swirls, one each in lime green,
blue and yellow braid, on the front of the pink jacket at the
upper left and lower right. Iron into place.

2 Heat-set 1 rhinestone to the center of each swirl
(pink rhinestone to green swirl, blue rhinestone to
yellow swirl, purple rhinestone to blue swirl).

3 Repeat steps 1 and 2 for the center back of the jacket,
using the photo on page 47 as a reference.

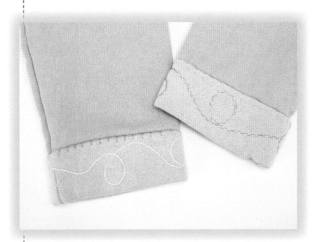

4 Blanket stitch 1 cuff with 6 strands of green floss or
1 strand of green pearl cotton, the other with yellow
floss or pearl cotton. Use the remaining yellow braid to
create a swirl extending into a loose curve across the cuff
with green blanket stitching. Trim the braid and iron
into place. Repeat with lime green braid on the cuff with
yellow blanket stitching.

Retro Dot Tunic

A small piece of retro dot fabric plus a worn-out sweatshirt evolves into a casual tunic to throw over a pair of jeans or white capris.

Super comfortable with an easy fit, this tunic glides over a larger waist. Buttons in cool colors punch up the retro dot pattern with funky flair.

Finished length: 24" (61cm).

Fit and Style

Create this tunic in brown and cream for a sophisticated look. Add a punch of color with a pin in red leather. Framing the face and neck is always very flattering.

Inspiration Board for *Retro Dot Tunic*

See the size and measurement guide on page 8 and compare the measurements of the sweatshirt you're using.

Back View of
Retro Dot Tunic

PATTERNS TO BE PRINTED FROM CD:

Curve guide (Sheet #0-A01)

Front panel pieces 1-5 (Sheets #3-B01, #3-B02, #3-B03, #3-B04, #3-B05)

Small circle pin template (Sheet #3-B06)

Front sweatshirt piece (Sheet #3-B07)

CUTTING PLAN

Cut two 4" × 13" (10cm × 33cm) cuff pieces from dot fabric.

Cut 1 pin piece from dot fabric.

Cut 2 front panel pieces from dot fabric.

Cut 1 front sweatshirt piece from the cutoff section of the green sweatshirt.

Cut 1 bottom band from a yellow sweatshirt (neck ruffle).

Cut the Sweatshirt

1 Refer to the *Inspiration Board* on page 51 for the project cutting diagram. Cut the cuffs and neckband from the green sweatshirt. Measure and cut 6" off the ends of the sleeves.

2 Measure 1" (25mm) down from the left underarm seam and 8" (20cm) down from the right underarm seam. Draw a line connecting these 2 points and cut along this line. Put this cut section aside for the front sweatshirt piece

Sew the Neck Ruffle

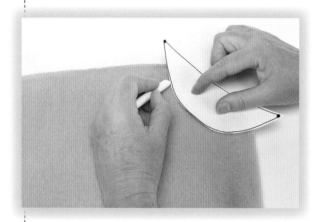

1 With the sweatshirt front folded in half, place the curve guide along the neck edge and draw a curve. Cut along this line.

2 Measure the yellow sweatshirt bottom band piece against the cut neck edge to check for fit. Stretch slightly to fit if needed.

3 Leave a ⅜" (9mm) back seam allowance on each end of the yellow band before pinning. Beginning at the center back or shoulder seam of the tunic, pin the open side of the yellow band to the neck edge.

4 Sew the yellow band to the neck edge, then topstitch another line ½" (13mm) from the seam line.

5 Leaving the casing open, sew a ⅜" (9mm) back seam on the yellow band and finish the edges.

Finish the Sleeves

1 Fold each cuff piece in half lengthwise with right sides together.

2 Sew all sides of each cuff piece, leaving a 2" (5cm) opening for turning. Clip the corners on each cuff, turn and press.

3 Pin the cuffs to the ends of the sleeves on the right side, matching the edges of the cuffs to the underarm seam lines. Topstitch the cuffs on all 4 sides.

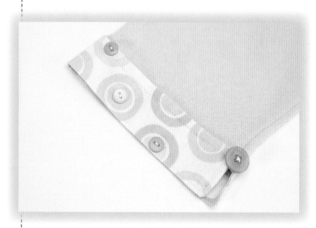

4 Sew six ⅜" (9mm) buttons, 3 of each color, to random dots on each cuff.

5 Sew a ⅝" (16mm) blue button to each cuff at the seam line.

Sew the Front Panel

1 Align the dot fabric front panel pieces, wrong sides together, and sew on 3 sides, leaving the fourth side open as indicated on the pattern. Clip the corners, turn and press.

2 Align the dot front panel piece to the diagonally trimmed sweatshirt front, matching raw edges. Sew and press.

3 Cut the front pattern piece from the discarded green sweatshirt piece. Pin to the side seam of the tunic and sew.

4 Pin the front pattern (sweatshirt) piece to the wrong side of the dot front panel piece.

5 Topstitch the dot front panel piece through the press seams. Sew ⅜" (9mm) buttons of each color to dots on the panel front (reserve 1 yellow button for the pin).

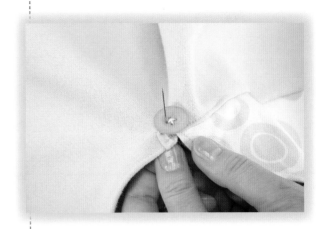

6 Sew one ⅝" (16mm) blue button where the panel meets the sweatshirt.

Finish the Neck Ruffle

1 Use a safety pin to thread elastic through the neck casing. Try the tunic on to determine how tight the elastic should be and adjust as needed.

2 Cut the elastic and sew the ends together. Slide the sewn ends of the elastic into the seam and finish the seam.

Make the Pin

1 Press the dotted pin fabric ¼" (6mm) under all the way around and baste into place.

2 Position the round wood piece in the center of the fabric circle. Pull the stitches tight and secure the threads.

3 Sew the pin back to the gathered fabric on the back and sew a ⅜" (9mm) yellow button to the center front of the pin.

Artsy Attitude Sweatshirt

Graphics printed onto photo transfer fabric punch up this clever statement for the "artist of the cloth." Snappy trim accentuates this sewing-themed sweatshirt and frames the mannequin graphics.

It takes only a simple sweatshirt, an iron and a few minutes to give this plain-jane sweatshirt a new look. Love to sew? Let it show!

Finished length: 21" (53cm).

Fit and Style

Interesting, attractive graphics and trim transform a plain sweatshirt quickly and easily. Use the same images to make a simple shopping bag to carry on quick trips to the market (or fabric store).

Artsy Attitude
Sweatshirt L
Detail punches it up
Comfort and style

No cutting required

Inspiration Board for *Artsy Attitude Sweatshirt*
See the size and measurement guide on page 8 and compare the measurements of the sweatshirt you're using.

Back View of
Artsy Attitude Sweatshirt

PATTERNS TO BE PRINTED FROM CD:

Mannequin graphics (Transfer Sheets #1 and #2)

CUTTING PLAN

Cut the mannequin graphics from the printed ink-jet fabric sheets.

Prepare the Sweatshirt

1 Refer to the *Inspiration Board* for this project on page 55—you'll see there are no cuts to be made to this sweatshirt.

2 Fold the cuffs of the sweatshirt to the inside of the sleeves to create sleeve facings.

Add the Trim

1 Measure the snap trim, adding ½" (13mm) to the measurement for each sleeve, and cut.

2 Pin the trim along the fold where the cuffs were turned inside the sleeves, folding the raw ends ¼" (6mm) under at the underarm seams. Sew through both the trim and the turned-in cuffs.

3 Measure the stitch line around the bottom band and add ½" (13mm). Cut a piece of trim to this measurement.

4 Pin the trim to the sweatshirt bottom band using the stitch line as a guide and sew into place.

Apply the Graphics

1 Iron to fuse the 3-mannequin graphic to the front of the sweatshirt.

2 Starting in 1 corner of the graphic, pin snap trim along the border, mitering the corners.

Embellish the Back

Add a graphic to the back of the sweatshirt for extra flair. Choose a favorite photo or photos for a different look. The CD that accompanies this book has an additional sewing-themed graphic design that can be used in creating this sweatshirt.

3 Cut the excess trim, leaving ¼" (6mm) to turn under at the final corner.

4 Sew the trim into place.

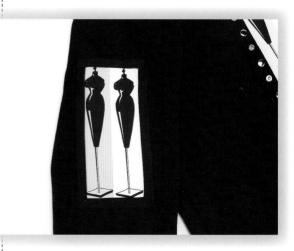

5 Iron to fuse the 2-mannequin graphic to the right sweatshirt sleeve.

6 Starting in 1 corner, pin black bias tape to edge the graphic, mitering the corners.

7 Trim the excess bias tape, leaving ¼" (6mm) to turn under at the final corner.

8 Sew the bias tape into place.

YOU WILL NEED

1 white sweatshirt

1 pink sweatshirt

1 fat quarter animal print fabric

1 fat quarter coordinating floral fabric

1 yd. (91cm) each pearl cotton (pink and white)

1½ yds. (1.3m) each ⅜"-wide (9mm) single-fold bias tape (pink and white)

Eight ⅞" (22mm) circle beads (lilac)

Five ⅝" (16mm) bright buttons (1 white, 2 purple, 2 pink)

Cutting mat

Embroidery needle

Iron and board

Large ruler

Matching and contrasting thread

Pins

Quilt pencil or chalk (white)

Rotary cutter

Scissors

Sewing machine

Chic Chica! Vest

Bright and full of festive color, this vibrant vest cleverly combines two sweatshirts, fun fat quarter yo-yos and brilliant buttons for sassy chica style.

This vest was inspired by the Crafty Chica Kathy Cano-Murillo, a very talented artist who creates on the run. (Once she was on her way out the door for a crafty event when she took scissors to her T-shirt to restyle it.) Her style is bold and colorful, just like this vivacious vest!

Finished length: 21" (53cm).

Fit and Style

Color blocking with length is always flattering. The eye is drawn to one color, which creates a slimmer visual. A simple solid color emphasizes that effect.

Inspiration Board for *Chic Chica! Vest*
See the size and measurement guide on page 8 and compare the measurements of the sweatshirt you're using.

**Back View of
*Chic Chica! Vest***

PATTERNS TO BE PRINTED FROM CD:

Large circle template (Sheet #0-D01)

CUTTING PLAN

Cut 3 yo-yos from the floral fabric.

Cut 2 yo-yos from the pink animal print fabric.

Cut two 7" (18cm) squares of pink animal print fabric. Draw a circle on the back of one square, but do not cut—the circle is sewn on the drawn line, then cut for the pocket.

Cut 2 pink sweatshirt circles from the trimmed sleeve for the front pieces.

Cut the Sweatshirt

1 Refer to the *Inspiration Board* on page 58 for the project cutting diagram. Measure ½" (13mm) beyond the armhole stitching line on the left side of the white sweatshirt and cut along this line. Repeat for the right side of the pink sweatshirt.

2 Cut the bottom bands from both sweatshirts.

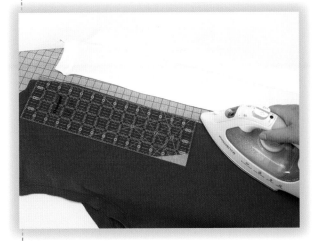

3 Measure and press the center lines of each sweatshirt and cut along these lines.

Don't Waste Those Sweatshirt Pieces

The second half of each sweatshirt can be used to create another garment with long sleeves. This is also a great design for using sweatshirts that have worn patches and stains.

Sew the Armholes

1 Press the armholes under ½"(13mm) on each sweatshirt half.

2 Topstitch the armholes with contrasting thread.

Sew the Pocket

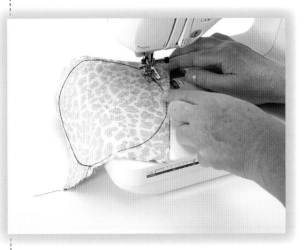

1 Place the 7" (18cm) squares of pink animal print fabric right sides together.

2 Sew around the entire drawn circle on the line, and trim to ¼" (6mm).

3 Measure 1" (25mm) from the edge and cut a 2" (5cm) slit through 1 layer of fabric only. Turn the pocket circle right side out and press.

4 Lay the circle with the slit side up and fold 2" (5cm) over to the front to hide the slit. Press and topstitch the folded edge.

5 Position the pocket 2½" (6cm) in from the left front edge of the vest and 2½" (6cm) up from the bottom. Pin into place.

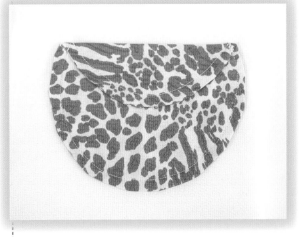

6 Topstitch the pocket to the vest.

Sew the Pink Front

1 Press both pink sweatshirt fabric circles in half with right sides together.

2 Sew around the curved side of each folded circle.

3 In each folded half circle, cut a small slit through 1 layer of fabric only just below the fold.

4 Turn each half circle right side out and press, then topstitch.

5 Press a ½" (13mm) hem from the neck edge to the back of the pink vest half.

6 Pin 1 folded pink half circle 3½" (9cm) down from the neck of the pink vest half, aligning with the pressed hem. Measure 1" (25mm) along the hem and pin a second half circle into place.

7 Fold pink bias tape over the raw edge of the pressed vest hem and pin into place. Topstitch with 2 rows of stitching ¼" (6mm) apart, sewing the pink half circles at the same time.

8 Press a ½" (13mm) hem from the neck edge to the back of the white vest half.

9 Repeat step 7 for the white vest half using white bias tape (there are no half circles on the white half.)

Make the Yo-Yos

1 Press ¼" (6mm) around the edges of 1 floral and 1 pink animal print fabric circle.

2 Sew the edges of the circles. Pull the threads tight on each and secure.

3 Press with the gathers centered.

4 Repeat to make 5 yo-yos in all (3 floral, 2 pink animal print).

5 Sew a button to the center of each yo-yo as follows: 1 pink button to the floral pocket yo-yo; 1 purple button each to the pink front floral yo-yo and animal print yo-yo; 1 pink button to the back floral yo-yo; and 1 white button to the back animal print yo-yo.

Sew the Back Seam

1 With wrong sides together, pin the white back seam to the pink back seam.

2 Sew the vest halves together. Trim the seam and press.

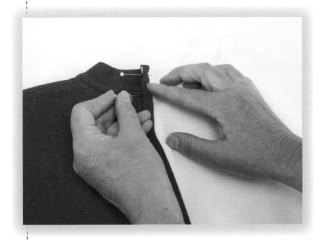

3 Pin pink bias tape 1" (25mm) over the neck edge, covering the white side of the back seam. Continue pinning along the right side seam, then topstitch into place.

4 Repeat step 3 with white bias tape, covering the pink side of the back seam.

Finish the Vest

1 Sew a floral yo-yo (with pink button) to the center of the pocket.

2 Sew 1 floral and 1 animal print yo-yo to the center of each pink front half circle.

3 Sew the remaining 2 yo-yos, spaced 1" (25mm) apart, centered over the bias tape on the lower back seam of the vest.

4 Stagger the circle beads 1½" (38mm) apart along the vest neckband and sew into place with pearl cotton. (Sew beads with pink pearl cotton on the white side of the vest; sew beads with white pearl cotton on the pink side of the vest.)

seasonal style

A man for all seasons is fine, but fabulous outerwear for all seasons is even better. In this chapter, comfort, warmth and sophisticated lines combine in projects that range from a fabulous fall cardigan to a rich, vibrant velvet coat for stepping out in style!

Luxurious velvet, textured wool and knits, sumptuous silk and extravagant fabric choices elevate these sweatshirt creations to designer fashion. An embroidery machine is useful for creating striking designs on fleece or velvet; however, for convenience you can purchase fabrics with embroidery and sequin details already in place. They may cost more, but if you shop the out-of-season clearance section at your local fabric store you can pick up some fabulous finds.

Vintage pieces from a thrift shop often yield gorgeous fabric patterns. If there isn't enough material for the garment you're making, consider using the pieces for the reverse appliqué technique. Finds like scarves and wool sweaters can be repurposed into garment accents and details. Assess each piece that catches your eye: Would it make a collar or cuffs?

You never know what might turn up as you shop or even travel. I found several sweaters and scarves on one recent trip. Wool felted up by hot machine washing and drying is as simple to work with as sweatshirt fleece. A single sweater yields a good size piece for felting if you cut open all of the seams.

YOU WILL NEED

1 navy sweatshirt

9" × 12" (23cm × 30cm) piece old gold wool felt

One 12" × 18" (30cm × 46cm) piece each wool felt in pumpkin, seagrass green and barnyard red

1 skein each pearl cotton in brown, rust and green

2 skeins gold pearl cotton

Fourteen ⅝" (16mm) buttons each in green and rust

Three 1" (25mm) navy buttons

Cutting mat

Embroidery needle

Iron and board

Large ruler

Matching thread

Quilt pencil or chalk (white)

Pins

Rotary cutter

Scissors

Sewing machine

Autumn Splendor Cardigan

A navy sweatshirt provides warmth and design contrast in this fall-inspired cardigan. Buttonhole details are worked into the cascade of richly colored wool felt maple leaves for ease of construction as well as design impact.

Cool autumn walks are a lot cozier in this beauty!

Finished length: 24" (61cm).

Fit and Style

This sweatshirt cardigan style is so easy to throw on when the air is chilly, and it's ideal for the autumn holiday season. For a more fitted look, use the curve C guide (Sheets #0-B01 and #0-B02 on the CD) for the back of the sweatshirt and narrow the side seams as well.

Autumn Splendor

Sweatshirt L

Slimming navy is punched up with rich wool tones

Cut open

7"

Cut

Cut

Cut off cuffs

Cut off cuffs

Cut off bottom band

Cut off cuffs

Inspiration Board for *Autumn Splendor Cardigan*
See the size and measurement guide on page 8 and compare the measurements of the sweatshirt you're using.

**Back View of
*Autumn Splendor Cardigan***

PATTERNS TO BE PRINTED FROM CD:

Curve guide (Sheet #0-A01)

Small and large leave templates (Sheet #4-A01)

CUTTING PLAN

Cut one 4" × 6" (10cm × 15cm) back tab piece from pumpkin wool felt.

Cut two 2" × 12" (5cm × 30cm) sleeve band pieces from pumpkin wool felt.

Cut 2 large and 3 small leaves from pumpkin wool felt.

Cut 4 large and 6 small leaves from barnyard red wool felt.

Cut 4 large and 7 small leaves from seagrass green wool felt.

Cut 4 small leaves from old gold wool felt.

Cut the Sweatshirt

1 Refer to the *Inspiration Board* on page 65 for the project cutting diagram. Carefully cut the bottom band and cuffs from the sweatshirt (the bottom band will be used as the front facing).

2 With the sweatshirt flat, right side out, measure 7" (18cm) over from the right side seam. Draw a chalk line from the neck edge to the lower sweatshirt edge at the 7" (18cm) mark. Cut the sweatshirt open along this line.

3 Use the curve guide to round off both bottom front corners of the sweatshirt.

Sew the Sweatshirt

1 Turn 1 end of the bottom band in ½" (13mm). Begin at the collar and pin the bottom band, right sides together, to the wider front of the sweatshirt.

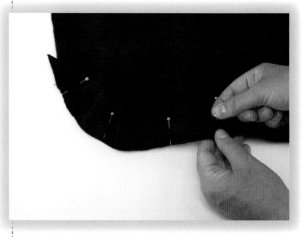

2 Pin around the front curve, stretching the sweatshirt only slightly. Taper the bottom band off at 2" (5cm) beyond the curved bottom of the sweatshirt. Trim off the excess band.

3 Sew the bottom band facing to the sweatshirt. Press and finish the seam.

4 Beginning at the opposite front neck of the sweatshirt, press ½" (13mm) under all the way around to the bottom band facing. Repeat for the sleeve ends.

5 Thread an embroidery needle with an 18–24" (46–61cm) length of gold pearl cotton. Beginning at the center back hem of the sweatshirt, blanket stitch the pressed edge around the entire sweatshirt. Continue across the edge of the neckband and band facing. Cut additional gold pearl cotton as needed.

6 Repeat this process for the sleeves.

Sew the Buttonhole Leaves

1 Match 1 pair each of red, green and pumpkin leaves. Align the edges and pin each pair together. Repeat for 1 pair of small gold leaves.

2 Blanket stitch around each large pair of leaves using rust pearl cotton for the green leaves, green pearl cotton for the red leaves and brown pearl cotton for the pumpkin leaves. Use brown pearl cotton to blanket stitch around the pair of small gold leaves. Stitches should be approximately 1/8" (3mm) in length and 1/4" (6mm) apart.

TIP: Begin the blanket stitch at the center bottom of a leaf, hiding the knot between the layers of felt.

3 Measure 1 1/2" (38mm) in from the tip of the large leaf. Draw a 1 1/4" (32mm) line and cut with sharp scissors to create a buttonhole. Repeat for the other 2 large leaves.

TIP: To make the leaves appear angled after they're sewn to the sweatshirt front, draw the line for the buttonhole at a slight angle.

4 Measure 1" (25mm) in from the tip of the small leaf. Draw a 1" (25mm) line and cut to create a buttonhole.

5 Blanket stitch or buttonhole stitch around each buttonhole, matching the color of pearl cotton used to blanket stitch around the edge of the leaf. (Make blanket stitches close together for a buttonhole stitch.)

6 Sew 1 rust button to the small gold leaf below the buttonhole.

7 Pin the small gold leaf to the neck at the end of the front facing. Make sure the buttonhole extends beyond the facing.

8 Pin the large leaves along the front edge, spaced 2" (5cm) apart, in this order: red, green and pumpkin. Make sure the buttonholes are straight and extend beyond the edge of the facing.

9 Stitching through the bottom layer of felt only, sew the leaves in place with matching thread.

10 Line up the front of the sweatshirt, overlapping the facing front. Pin and mark where the buttons should go on the left side of the front.

11 Sew 1 navy button for each of the 3 large buttonholes; sew 1 rust button on the shoulder for the small buttonhole.

Appliqué the Leaves

1 Refer to the photo for step 11 above to arrange and pin small leaves in between the buttonhole leaves along the front: 2 green, 2 red, 2 pumpkin.

2 Along the neck, pin 1 small pumpkin, red, green and gold leaf. Pin a red and a green leaf to finish off the back neck edge. Extend a couple of leaves beyond the neck edge and trim off the excess.

3 Blanket stitch all of the leaves in place using rust pearl cotton for the green leaves, green pearl cotton for the red leaves and brown pearl cotton for the pumpkin and gold leaves.

4 Sew alternating pairs of rust and green buttons to every other small leaf.

Finish the Sleeves

1 Measure 2" (5cm) up from the sleeve end. Pin 1 end of the pumpkin band piece at the sleeve seam.

2 Try on the sweatshirt. Pull the unpinned band end around the sleeve to the pinned end, overlapping where it is comfortable. Mark this point with a pin.

3 Remove the sweatshirt and unpin the band. Cut the band off 2" (5cm) beyond the pin mark. Repeat for the second band piece.

4 Measure ½" (13mm) from 1 end of each of the sleeve band pieces. Mark and cut 1" (25mm) lines for buttonholes.

5 Blanket stitch with brown pearl cotton around the buttonholes in each band.

6 Blanket stitch around all 4 edges of each sleeve band with brown pearl cotton. Sew the ends of the bands to the sleeve seams.

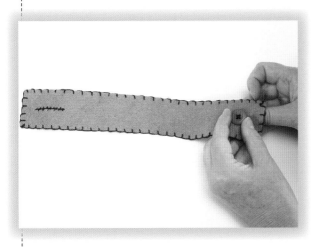

Sew the Back Tab

1 Fold the pumpkin back tab piece in half lengthwise. Blanket stitch on all 4 sides with brown pearl cotton.

2 Align and pin together 1 pair each of small red and green leaves. Blanket stitch around the edges of each pair.

3 Measure down 11" (28cm) from the center back top edge of the sweatshirt and pin the center of the back tab at this mark.

7 Sew a green button to 1 band end and a rust button to the other band end at the sleeve seam.

8 Align and pin a pair of large red and green leaves together. Blanket stitch around the edges of each pair.

9 Pin a small gold leaf to the center of the green leaves and a small green leaf to the center of the red leaves. Blanket stitch into place.

10 Sew 2 rust buttons to the small green leaf and 2 green buttons to the small gold leaf centers.

11 Pin the top and bottom of the leaves to the center of the sleeve fronts with the tips just above the blanket-stitched sleeve edge.

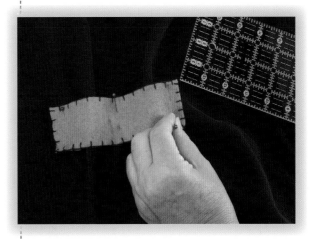

4 Fold an extra 1" (25mm) of sweatshirt fabric into each side under the back tab. Pin the back tab on each end.

5 Try on the sweatshirt for fit. Add or remove extra fabric under the tab ends as needed.

6 Pin a leaf to either end of the tab. Sew a pair of rust buttons to the green leaf and a pair of green buttons to the red leaf to hold the tab in place.

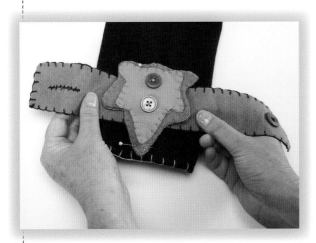

12 Insert the sleeve bands between the pinned leaves and sleeves.

13 With matching thread, stitch leaves at the bottom and top through their backs only. Don't catch the sleeve bands so they'll move when unbuttoned.

YOU WILL NEED

1 burgundy sweatshirt

1 yd. (91cm) embroidered teal velvet

1¾ yds. (1.6m) burgundy velvet

2 yds. (1.8m) fabric for lining

1 yd. (91cm) iron-on interfacing

Fabric glue

1¼" (32mm) button

½ yd. (46cm) each of ¼"-wide (6mm) satin ribbon in teal, gold and burgundy

Cutting mat

Iron and board

Long quilting ruler or yardstick

Matching thread

Needle

Pins

Quilt pencil or chalk (white)

Rotary cutter

Scissors

Sewing machine

Fine Wine Coat

Many of today's fabric choices are detailed with stunning embroidery and embellishment. For the home sewer, this raises garment-making to another level.

Rich velvet with contrasting embroidery and sequins elevates this plain sweatshirt to a luxurious coat for a special evening out, or wear it to holiday parties or to the office paired with a wool scarf and leather gloves.

Finished length: 36" (91cm).

Fit and Style

An A-line cut and empire waist create a style that is flattering as well as comfortable. For a holiday event, add a beautiful pashmina for instant elegance.

Use collar pattern to trim

Cut open

Cut

Cut open side seams

Cut off cuffs

Cut off cuffs

Cut off bottom band

Cut off cuffs

Fine Wine

Sweatshirt L

Coat style lengthens body

Slims hips

Inspiration Board for *Fine Wine Coat*
See the size and measurement guide on page 8 and compare the measurements of the sweatshirt you're using.

Back View of
Fine Wine Coat

PATTERNS TO BE PRINTED FROM CD:

Curve C guide 1 and 2 (Sheet #0-B01 and #0-B02)

Collar pieces 1, 2 and 3 (Sheets #4-B01, #4-B02, #4-B03)

CUTTING PLAN

Cut two 16" × 25" (41cm × 63cm) front pieces from burgundy velvet.

Cut one 25" × 26" (64cm × 66cm) back piece from burgundy velvet.

Cut two 16" × 25" (41cm × 63cm) front pieces from lining fabric.

Cut one 25" × 26" (64cm × 66cm) back piece from lining fabric.

Cut two 4" × 31" (10cm × 79cm) front trim pieces from teal velvet.

Cut two 9" × 12½" (23cm × 32cm) cuff pieces from teal velvet.

Cut 1 upper collar piece from teal velvet.

Cut 1 under collar piece from lining fabric.

Cut 1 collar piece from interfacing.

Cut the Sweatshirt

1 Refer to the *Inspiration Board* on page 71 for the project cutting diagram. Cut the bottom band and cuffs from the sweatshirt.

2 Cut the sweatshirt open along the side seams. Measure 5" (13cm) down from the underarm seams; cut the sweatshirt off along the line between these points.

3 Measure to find the center front of the sweatshirt and cut open.

4 Use the lower 2 collar pattern pieces (#4-B02 and #4-B03) to trim the neckline. Place the collar pattern along the front of the sweatshirt extending from the shoulder seam to the front edge; align the shoulder seam with the dotted line at the top of #4-B02. Draw a line along the inner collar edge between these points. Repeat for the opposite side, then cut along both lines.

TIP: The line will cut off some of the neckband; the remainder will be used to finish off the underside of the collar.

Sew the Collar

1 Fuse interfacing to the wrong side of the collar lining piece. Match the velvet collar and lining pieces with right sides together and pin.

2 Sew all around the collar with a ½" (13mm) seam allowance, leaving a 2" (5cm) opening in the center top to turn.

3 Trim the corners and finish the seam. Turn the collar and press.

4 Topstitch the collar along the sides and upper edge; do not topstitch the lower edge.

5 Pin the bottom edge of the right side of the collar to the wrong side of the lower edge of the neckband. Sew along the bottom edge of the collar using the topstitch line as a guide. Press the seam.

6 Flip the collar to the right side of the jacket.

TIP: This technique gives the collar body.

7 Hand-stitch the neckband to the collar lining; this gives the underside of the collar a finished look.

Sew the Cuffs

1 Try the jacket on to check the sleeve length. Trim the sleeve, if necessary. The cuff extends over the sleeve edge, so it can be adjusted for arm length.

2 Press a 1¾" (44mm) hem on 1 long side of each cuff piece. Press a ½" (13mm) hem on the opposite long side of each cuff piece. Leave the cuff hems unstitched until you sew the jacket.

Cutting Strategy

In working with this embroidered velvet, I cut the cuff pieces from the selvage end of the fabric, which had an extra design row of sequins.

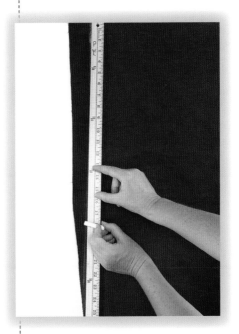

3 Pin the cuffs to the sleeves, with the cuffs extending 2" (5cm) from the sleeve ends. The cuff ends meet at the underarm seam. Topstitch the cuffs into place.

Cut the Lower Coat

1 Lay 1 burgundy velvet front piece flat with the wrong side up.

3 Line up the ruler from the bottom outside edge of the front piece to the mark at the top. Cut along this diagonal line for the side seam line.

2 Measure 2" (5cm) in from 1 outside edge at the top of the front piece and mark.

4 Using the trimmed side of the front piece as a pattern guide, cut the opposite front piece side seam as well as the back and side seam lines.

5 Repeat steps 1–4 to cut the lining pieces.

Sew the Coat Pieces

1 Align the back coat pieces with right sides together, pinning the lower coat to the upper coat. Sew, finish the seam and press.

2 Align the lower front pieces to the lower coat pieces at the side seams and sew the lower coat to the upper coat.

Sew the Curve C Seams

1 Lay the coat completely flat with the wrong side facing up. Place the curve C guide along the sleeve stitch line at the back. Draw a line along the curve, using the long ruler to extend the line the full length of the lower coat back. Repeat for the opposite side of the back.

2 Fold the jacket along this line with right sides together. Measure ¼" (6mm) from the fold and mark at the upper coat seam line. Pin, narrowing until even with the sleeve stitch line and lower coat at the opposite end. Sew along this line.

3 Repeat for the opposite curve. The seam can be made larger, if needed, by adding another ¼" (6mm) to the seam measurement; narrow to the sleeve seam as described in step 2.

4 Press the curved seams toward the side seams.

Sew the Side Seams

1 Fold the coat with right sides together along the underarm seam line. At the seam line on the side seam, measure 1" (25mm) in and mark.

2 From this point draw a line narrowing to ½" (13mm), the regular seam width, at either end of the seam. Pin along this line.

3 Try the coat on before continuing. If the coat is not fitted enough, add another ¼" (6mm) to the measurement and redraw the line. If the coat is too tight, reduce the line by ¼" (6mm).

4 Sew and finish the seams.

Sew the Lining

1 Align the back and front lining pieces and pin. Sew the lining pieces together.

2 Press a ½" (13mm) hem to the wrong side along the top of the lining.

3 Pin the lining to the coat with right sides together. Sew on 3 sides. Turn the lining to the inside of the coat and press.

4 Press the bodice seam over the lining top and pin. Topstitch the seam with 3 rows ⅛" (3mm) apart.

5 Press a 1½" (38mm) bottom hem. Topstitch along the top edge of the hem with 2 rows ¼" (6mm) apart. This will hold the lining in place neatly.

Sew the Front Trim

1 Measure in 2" (5cm) at the top of each trim piece. Draw a line from the bottom to this mark on each piece and cut.

2 Press in ½" (13mm) along all sides of the trim pieces. Press each piece in half lengthwise with wrong sides together.

3 Measure the coat length from the collar end. Fold the hems of the trim pieces so their length matches the coat length. Press.

4 Align the bottom of the trim and the coat hem, extending the trim 1½" (38mm) beyond the edge of the coat front. Pin the straight side of the trim to the front edge of the coat and topstitch on all 4 sides.

Use the Trim to Adjust the Fit

The trim could be sewn closer to the front coat edge for a roomier fit, or a wider trim can be cut if needed. Simply adjust it to the size of your hips.

Finish the Button

1 Braid the 3 colors of satin ribbon tightly. Beginning at the center of the button, glue the braided ribbon in a spiral. Cover the entire button. When the glue is dry, trim the ends of the ribbon.

2 Sew a snap at the end of the collar. Sew the button to the front of the trim at the end of the collar.

YOU WILL NEED

1 purple sweatshirt

1 burgundy wool sweater

One 9" × 12" (23cm × 30cm) piece cream wool felt

One 9" × 12" (23cm × 30cm) piece denim wool felt

One 9" × 12" (23cm × 30cm) piece teal wool felt

One 10" × 52" (25cm × 132cm) wool plaid scarf

1 skein each embroidery floss or 1 ball each pearl cotton in burgundy and teal

Cutting mat

Embroidery needle

Iron and board

Large ruler

Matching thread

Pins

Rotary cutter

Scissors

Sewing machine

Cozy Knit Jacket

This cozy jacket combines warm wool and touches of purple for a topper that goes great with jeans. A recycled felted sweater and trendy scarf make the knit accents super fast and simple to create.

Thrift store visits always result in a stash of clothing to repurpose. Wool sweaters are especially prized—they can be felted quickly by machine-washing and -drying.

Finished length: 22" (56cm).

Fit and Style

This softly shaped jacket draws the emphasis upward with flattering scarf and collar details around the face. The gentle lines of this cozy wearable camouflage a thicker waistline.

Cut open

Cut off cuffs

Cut off bottom band

Cut off cuffs

Cut off cuffs

Cozy Knit

Sweatshirt S

Scarf cozy style detail

Bright accent color

Inspiration Board for *Cozy Knit Jacket*

See the size and measurement guide on page 8 and compare the measurements of the sweatshirt you're using.

Back View of
Cozy Knit Jacket

PATTERNS TO BE PRINTED FROM CD:

Small/medium/large square templates (Sheet #4-C01)

CUTTING PLAN

Cut 7"-wide (18cm) collar piece from the sweater bottom.*

Cut 2 cuff pieces from the sweater* 1" (25mm) above the ribbing.

Cut two 4" × 20" (10cm × 51cm) band pieces from the sweater.*

Cut two 4" × 24" (10cm × 61cm) front trim pieces from the scarf.

Cut two 4" × 27" (10cm × 69cm) back scarf pieces from the scarf.

Cut 1 S, 2 M and 2 L squares from teal wool felt.

Cut 1 S, 2 M and 1 L square from denim wool felt.

Cut 2 S and 2 M squares from cream wool felt.

Felt the sweater before cutting.

Cut the Sweatshirt

1 Refer to the *Inspiration Board* on page 77 for the project cutting diagram. Cut the cuffs and the bottom band from the sweatshirt; leave the neckband for a closer-fitting collar.

2 Fold the sweatshirt in half lengthwise, press and cut open along the center front fold.

Felt the Sweater

1 Machine-wash the sweater in hot water.

2 Machine-dry the sweater.

TIP: Felting a sweater also keeps it from unraveling as the fibers are matted together.

Sew the Cuffs and the Lower Band

1 With right sides together, stretch the wool sweater cuffs over the ends of the sweatshirt sleeves, aligning the raw edges, and sew.

2 With right sides together, sew the sweater band pieces to make a 4"× 39" (10cm × 99cm) band. Press the front trim pieces in half and sew. Trim the seams and press.

Sew the Front Scarf Trim

1 Fold 1 front trim piece in half with wrong sides together and press.

2 Pin the trim to the front edge of the jacket with the fringe extending beyond the jacket bottom edge.

3 Repeat with the second front trim piece for the opposite jacket front.

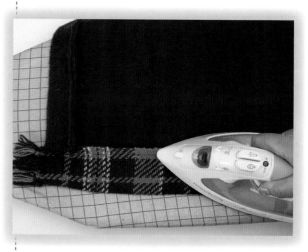

4 Sew, finish the seam and press. Cut any excess trim even with the neck edge.

Sew the Collar

1 Measure the sweater collar piece against the neck edge. The sweater collar piece should extend 2" (5cm) beyond the neckline.

2 Press a ½" (13mm) hem on either end of the collar piece, then fold and press another ½" (13mm). Pin to hold.

3 Pin the right side of the collar piece to the wrong side of the sweatshirt along the edge of the neckband. Sew into place and trim the seam.

4 Pin the neck ribbing of the sweatshirt to the underside of the collar. Hand-sew into place.

Sewing the Scarf

1 Align the short ends of the remaining scarf pieces. Sew together and press.

2 Fold the scarf in half lengthwise with right sides together. Sew on all 3 sides leaving a 3" (8cm) opening to turn. Turn the scarf and hand-sew the opening closed.

3 Sew a 4½" (11cm) loop of burgundy floss or pearl cotton under the collar at the center of the finished neck. Insert the scarf through the loop, centering evenly.

Applying the Appliqué Squares

1 Using the photo above and on page 76 as a reference, position the felt squares on the front of the jacket as shown. Pin into place.

2 With 3 strands of burgundy embroidery floss or 1 strand of burgundy pearl cotton, sew a running stitch around each square.

3 Repeat steps 1–2 for the appliquéd square design on the back of the jacket, using the photo above and on page 77 as a reference.

Finishing Stitches

1 Using 6 strands of teal embroidery floss or 1 strand of teal pearl cotton, sew 2 rows of running stitches ¼" (6mm) apart on the lower knit band.

2 Repeat step 1 for both knit cuffs.

3 Repeat step 1 for all 3 sides of the knit collar. Add 1 additional row of running stitches to the short ends of the collar.

YOU WILL NEED

1 white sweatshirt

3 yds. (2.7m) striped knit

1 yd. (91cm) silk with large floral pattern

1½ yds. (1.4m) iron-on interfacing

Three 2" (5cm) metal clasps

Basting stick (fabric glue stick)

Cutting mat

Iron and board

Large ruler

Matching thread

Needle

Pins

Quilt pencil or chalk (white)

Rotary cutter

Scissors

Sewing machine

Small pointed scissors

Classy Gal! Coat

This classy coat, with versatile sleeve design and dressy reverse silk appliqués, is the smart answer for breezy spring days. Sweatshirt fleece works well with reverse appliqué (see page 86 for a special demonstration of this technique). You can incorporate beautiful silk prints and other fancy materials into this design; simply back them with stabilizer for extra durability.

Finished length: 42" (107cm).

Fit and Style

The added sleeve gives this coat a fitted shoulder. The sweatshirt sleeve can be removed for a lighter feel or made detachable for more versatility.

I wore this coat to the International Quilt Market, and many women commented on it. They asked if I made it and couldn't believe it was a sweatshirt!

Inspiration Board for *Classy Gal! Coat*
See the size and measurement guide on page 8 and compare the measurements of the sweatshirt you're using.

Back View of
Classy Gal! Coat

PATTERNS TO BE PRINTED FROM CD:

Collar pieces 1 and 2 (Sheets #0-C01 and #0-C02)

Sleeve pieces 1 and 2 (Sheets #4-D01 and #4-D02)

CUTTING PLAN

Cut two 17" × 37" (43cm × 94cm) front pieces from striped knit.

Cut one 29" × 37" (74cm × 94cm) back piece from striped knit.

Cut two 3½" × 11½" (9cm × 29cm) cuff pieces from striped knit.

Cut two 3½" × 12" (9cm × 30cm) front trim pieces from striped knit.

Cut one 3½" × 40" (9cm × 102cm) belt piece from striped knit.

Cut 2 sleeve pieces from striped knit.

Cut 2 collar pieces* from striped knit.

Cut 8 large flower motifs** from silk floral fabric.

*Apply interfacing to 1 collar piece according to manufacturer's instructions before cutting.

**Apply interfacing to the silk according to manufacturer's instructions before cutting.

Cut the Sweatshirt

1 Refer to the *Inspiration Board* on page 81 for the project cutting diagram. Cut the sweatshirt open along the side seams.

2 Measure 5" (13cm) down from the underarm seams and cut the sweatshirt off along this line.

3 Measure to find the center front and cut open along this line.

Sew the Cuffs

1 Press the sweatshirt cuff under ½" (13mm).

2 Fold each striped knit cuff piece in half with right sides together; sew only the long side.

3 Turn each cuff piece and press with the seam centered underneath. Pin each cuff ¼" (6mm) from a sleeve end and topstitch into place.

Sew the Front Trim

1 Press 1 long side of each striped knit front trim piece under ½" (13mm).

2 Press each front trim piece in half.

3 Pin the front trim pieces over the raw front edges of the sweatshirt top and topstitch into place.

Sew the Collar

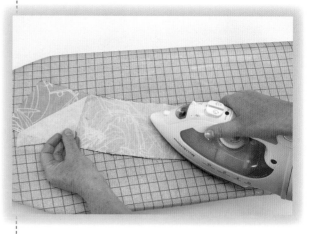

1 Apply interfacing to the underside of the striped knit collar piece only. Match the collar pieces with right sides together and pin.

2 Sew all around the collar with a ½" (13mm) seam allowance, leaving a 2" (5cm) opening in the center top to turn.

3 Trim the corners and finish the seam. Turn the collar and press.

4 Topstitch the collar along 2 sides and the top; do not topstich the lower edge.

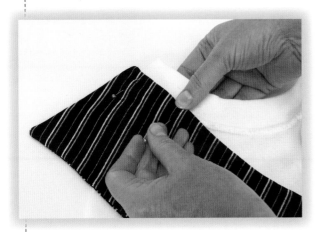

5 Pin the right side lower edge of the collar to the wrong side lower edge of the neckband.

6 Sew the collar to the neckband along the lower edge of the collar with a ¼" (6mm) seam. Press the seam.

7 Flip the collar to the right side of the coat. This technique gives the collar body.

8 Fold over the neck ribbing and stitch to the neck seam line to give it a finished look.

Cut the Lower Coat

1 Lay 1 striped knit front piece flat with the wrong side up.

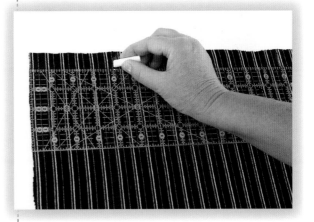

2 At the top of the piece, measure in 4" (10cm) from the outside edge and mark.

3 Line up the ruler from the bottom outside edge of the striped knit front piece to the mark at the top.

4 Cut along this diagonal line for the side seam line.

5 Use this cut side of the striped knit front piece as a pattern for cutting the opposite front side seam as well as the back and side seam lines.

Sew Coat Pieces

1 Align the front and back side seams and sew. Finish the seams and press.

2 Measure the upper edge of the lower coat against the bodice. The lower coat should extend 2" (5cm) on either side of the bodice to create front facings.

TIP: If the sweatshirt is wider and there is not enough of the lower coat to extend for facings, cut 2 strips of striped knit fabric the same length as the coat before hemming: sew to both sides of the lower front to create the facings.

3 Press ¼" (6mm) under on long sides of facing raw edges and press 1¾" (44mm) under to create facings. Topstitch.

4 Align the side seams and front of the sweatshirt bodice with the lower coat, and pin.

5 Sew, finish the seam and press.

6 Press the bottom edge of the lower coat ½" (13mm) under, then 2" (5cm) under again for the hem and topstitch.

Sew the Belt

1 Fold the belt in half lengthwise. Sew the sides, leaving a 3" (8cm) center opening to turn. Press the belt after turning.

2 Center the belt along the seam line, aligning with the front edge. Pin the belt to both front sections of the coat to 2" (5cm) beyond the underarm seams.

3 Topstitch the belt, leaving the center back free.

4 Pin the center of the belt to the center back of the coat. Tack into place.

TIP: The belt is left loose at the back to gather the coat slightly for a better fit. If you want the belt tighter, shorten the length of the belt before sewing it to the coat.

Choosing Fabric for Reverse Appliqué

Fabric used for reverse appliqué needs to be printed so the design shows on both the right and wrong sides to allow for accurate stitching.

For large reverse appliqué elements, or when using a lighter fabric like silk, apply lightweight fusible interfacing to the fabric before cutting out the elements. You will be able to see the outline of the design, but the interfacing will make the garment sturdier.

Sew the Reverse Appliqué Flowers

1 See *Doing Reverse Appliqué* on page 86. Prepare the silk flower appliqué motifs

2 Starting with the front of the coat, position and pin the prepared flower motifs (or use a basting stick) with right sides facing the wrong side of coat. Use the photo on page 80 as a reference.

3 Carefully stitch each flower appliqué to the coat.

4 Repeat steps 2–3 for the back of the coat (use the photo on page 81 as a reference). Also apply 1 flower reverse appliqué on each striped sleeve.

5 Pull the center of each appliquéd flower away from the fabric while piercing the right side of the fabric carefully with sharp-pointed scissors. Cut closely through the fabric along the stitch line around each appliquéd flower. Remove the trimmed fabric to reveal the appliqué.

DOING REVERSE APPLIQUÉ

Reverse appliqué is a great technique for sweatshirt designs. The sweatshirt fabric will not fray, and the topstitching around the design can be a nice contrast. Design elements are cut from fabric with a ½" (13mm) border and sewn from the wrong side of the sweatshirt.

1 Carefully cut the design element from fabric with sharp scissors, leaving a ¼" (6mm) to ½" (13mm) border around each one.

2 Apply a basting stick (fabric glue stick) to the border on the right side of the appliqué design. Affix the element to wrong side of the sweatshirt in the desired location. (The right side of the appliqué should be against the wrong side of the sweatshirt fabric.)

3 With small stitches, carefully sew around each element.

4 Pull the center of the element away from the sweatshirt where the sweatshirt fabric covers the appliqué. At the same time, pierce the right side of the sweatshirt carefully with scissors.

5 With sharp-pointed scissors, closely cut the right side of the sweatshirt along the stitch line around each appliqué element.

6 Remove the trimmed sweatshirt piece to reveal the appliqué.

Finish the Sleeves

1 Press ½" (13mm) under around the curve of each striped sleeve.

2 Press a ½" (13mm) hem on each striped sleeve and topstitch.

3 Fold the sleeves in half lengthwise and sew. Turn and press.

4 Try on the coat. Mark the center shoulder line with a pin.

5 Pull the striped sleeves over the sweatshirt sleeves, aligning the underarm seams. Bring the striped sleeves to the shoulder line.

6 Pin the striped sleeves along the curve with the underarm seams aligned.

7 Sew the sleeves in place by machine or by hand.

Add the Closures

1 Sew 1 closure to each coat front at the belt.

2 Measure 3½" (9cm) on either side of the center closure to position the remaining closures and sew into place.

recycled? remarkable!

So often great pieces of clothing are discarded for a variety of reasons, but they can be rescued and restyled into eye-catching fashions.

I must confess this is my favorite chapter. I was able to use some pieces of clothing I liked but considered unwearable. Every time I opened my closet, there they were, looking at me longingly as I guiltily shut the door. Okay, a slight exaggeration, but they were a constant reminder—until I restyled them.

Many of us would rather not call attention to our midsections. A jacket that skims that area gives us a leaner outline. It also creates the illusion of a taller frame.

Restyling a sweatshirt into an attractive shape and combining other garment pieces is good for the environment—your personal space as well as the world's. Your closet will be lighter—and a well-fitting outfit always makes us *feel* lighter. Thrift store finds, closet rejects and our curiously shrinking garments cry out for new life. Mixing in fabric remnants and trims results in some very cool pieces to wear. Again, sweatshirts to the rescue—from recycled to remarkable!

YOU WILL NEED

1 denim sweatshirt

¼ yd. (23cm) yellow polka-dot fabric

¼ yd. (23cm) bold print fabric (for appliqué motifs)

1 blue jean remnant

1 package ½" (13mm) grommets (with included setting tool)

¼ yd. (23cm) fusible adhesive

1 yd. (91cm) ⅛"-wide (3mm) yellow ribbon

Cutting mat

Hammer

Iron and board

Large ruler

Matching and contrasting thread

Pins

Quilt pencil or chalk (white)

Rotary cutter

Scissors

Sewing machine

Denim Blues Vest

Frayed jean remnants, scrap fabric and a worn sweatshirt are revived in this casual pullover vest with fresh detailing. Wide shoulders on a sweatshirt, when altered, become the very trendy cap sleeve. Add a white shirt for tailored ease and great jeans to finish the look. Tie on a belt created simply from the cutoff bottom band of the sweatshirt. A fun, fresh look couldn't be easier!

Finished length: 24" (61cm).

Fit and Style

This vest can be worn with or without a belt. If you choose to wear the belt, tie it slightly above the natural waistline.

Inspiration Board for *Denim Blues Vest*
See the size and measurement guide on page 8 and compare the measurements of the sweatshirt you're using.

Back View of
Denim Blues Vest

PATTERNS TO BE PRINTED FROM CD:

Curve C guide 1 and 2 (Sheets #0-B01 and #0-B02)

Appliqué template (Sheet #5-A01)

CUTTING PLAN

Cut one 6½" (16cm) square of blue jean remnant for neck insert.

Cut 2 appliqué pieces (using template) from yellow polka-dot fabric.

Cut 3 appliqué motifs* from bold print fabric.

Apply fusible adhesive to the bold print fabric before cutting.

Cut the Sweatshirt

1 Refer to the *Inspiration Board* on page 91 for the project cutting diagram. Measure ½" (13mm) beyond the armhole stitching line and cut the sleeve along this line. Repeat for the other sleeve.

2 Carefully cut the bottom band from the sweatshirt with the stitching intact.

3 Cut the sweatshirt open along the side seams.

TIP: Cutting the side seams open so the sweatshirt lies flat makes it much easier to sew around the neckline and armholes.

4 Mark the center front of the sweatshirt at the neck. Measure 7" (18cm) from the neckband down the center of the sweatshirt. Angle a ruler to 1 side of the neckband at the shoulder seam and draw a line to the bottom of the center line. Repeat for the opposite side of the neck.

5 Cut along each of these lines, removing some of the neckband.

Sew the Curve C Back Seams

1 Lay the sweatshirt completely flat with the wrong side facing up. Align the curve C guide with the back armhole stitch line and draw a curved line to the bottom of the sweatshirt. Repeat for the opposite side of the back.

2 Fold the sweatshirt with right sides together along this line.

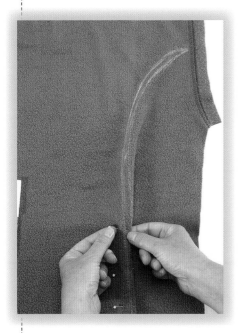

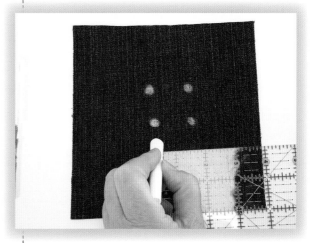

3 Measure ¼" (6mm) from this fold and mark at the lower sweatshirt edge. Pin, narrowing to the seam at the opposite end. Sew along this line. Repeat for the remaining curve.

Enlarging the Seam

The seam can also be made larger, if needed, by adding another ¼" (6mm) to the measurement; narrow the seam to the armhole as instructed.

4 Press both curved seams toward the side seams.

5 Topstitch ⅛" (3mm) from the curved seams on the right side of the sweatshirt.

Make the Neck Insert

1 Press the 6½" (16cm) blue jean square in half and mark the center. Unfold and lay flat.

2 Measure 2" (5cm) down from the top of the denim square. Mark ⅜" (9mm) on either side of the center fold line for the first pair of grommets.

3 Measure and mark 2 more pairs of grommets, with ⅝" (16mm) between each pair. Poke a small hole at each grommet mark.

4 Lay the denim square right side down on a flat, hard surface. Insert a grommet piece through a hole from underneath (the right side of the denim). Place a grommet washer over the grommet on the wrong side of the denim.

5 Use a hammer and the setting tool that comes pack-aged with the grommets to join the grommet pieces. Repeat for the remaining 5 holes.

6 Lace yellow ribbon through the grommets. Tie a bow, and trim the ends.

Sew the Neck Insert

1 Pin the wrong side of the denim neck piece to the right side of the yellow polka-dot piece; make sure the ends of the yellow ribbon are tucked in between the layers.

2 Sew all sides of the neck insert, leaving a 2" (5cm) opening in the bottom for turning.

3 Turn the neck insert and press the edges carefully.

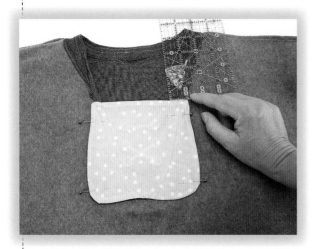

4 Pin the neck insert into the neckline of the sweat-shirt. Topstitch 2 rows ¼" (6mm) apart around the entire neckline and band.

Sew the Armhole

1 Press the raw edges of the sweatshirt armholes under to the stitch line.

2 Topstitch the armholes and press.

Affix the Appliqués

1 Pin the yellow polka-dot appliqué pieces with right sides together. Sew on all 4 sides, leaving an opening where indicated on the pattern.

2 Turn each appliqué piece right side out and press.

3 Pin the yellow polka-dot appliqué to the lower right side of the sweatshirt, matching the side seam and bottom. Topstitch in place along the curve.

4 Position 1 bold print appliqué motif slightly offset from the yellow polka-dot appliqué (see photo on page 90 for reference). Press to fuse the appliqué motif according to manufacturer's instructions.

5 Position the second appliqué offset at the left shoulder and the third appliqué offset at the back neckline (see photos on pages 90 and 91). Press to fuse to the sweatshirt.

Sew the Side Seams and Hem

1 Align the side seams of the sweatshirt with right sides together. Sew, finish the seams and press.

2 Press a ½" (13mm) hem along the bottom of the vest.

3 Topstitch 2 rows ¼" (6mm) apart along the hem. Trim and press.

Finish the Belt

1 Turn the bottom band that was cut from the sweat-shirt inside out

2 Press both ends in ½" (13mm) and stitch closed.

1 teal sweatshirt

6 ties

2 medium blue buttons (cuffs)

Cutting mat

Iron and board

Large ruler

Matching thread

Needle

Pins

Quilt pencil or chalk (white)

Rotary cutter

Scissors

Sewing machine

All Tied Up Tunic

At a small used clothing store I picked up a bunch of great ties for only ten cents apiece. The colorful patterns blend together in this terrific tie-trimmed tunic.

For an even cheaper option (and maybe even more fun), raid your husband's or boyfriend's tie collection. If there are no men in your life at the moment, go to the thrift store and give those secondhand ties a new life and stylish revamp!

Finished length: 25" (64cm).

Fit and Style

The flattering lines of an asymmetrical cut combined with neck detailing make this a good look for every figure. The silk ties add a dressy accent.

All Tied Up

Sweatshirt S

Silk ties add luxurious touch

Diagonal lines flattering

Cut

Cut

Cut

8"

8"

3½"

Cut off bottom band

Inspiration Board for *All Tied Up Tunic*

See the size and measurement guide on page 8 and compare the measurements of the sweatshirt you're using.

Back View of
All Tied Up Tunic

PATTERNS TO BE PRINTED FROM CD:

None

CUTTING PLAN

Cut four 3¼" × 25" (8cm × 63cm) bottom pieces from ties.

Cut four 2" × 11" (5cm × 28cm) sleeve band pieces from ties.

Cut two 3¼" × 22" (8cm × 56cm) neck pieces from ties.

Cut three 2" × 10" (5cm × 25cm) fabric rose pieces from ties.

Preparing the Sweatshirt

1 Refer to the *Inspiration Board* on page 96 for the project cutting diagram. Measure 8" (20cm) up from the cuff end of the inside seam of 1 sleeve. Draw a line from the cuff to this point and cut. Repeat for the second sleeve.

2 Cut the bottom band from the sweatshirt. Measure 3½" (9cm) from the bottom of the sweatshirt on 1 side seam. Draw a diagonal line from this point to the opposite bottom edge and cut along this line.

Sewing the Bottom

1 For the front, overlap the long sides of 2 tie pieces ½" (13mm), keeping the wide points at the same end; topstitch together. Repeat for the back with 2 additional tie pieces.

2 Align the topstitched tie pieces and sew the short ends together.

3 Pin the assembled tie piece bottom to the sweatshirt bottom, with the wider ends of the ties at the higher side of the sweatshirt bottom. Topstitch into place and press.

Sewing the Sleeve Trim

1 Sew 2 tie sleeve trim pieces together. Align the tie seams with the underarm seams and pin, overlapping the sleeve ½" (13mm).

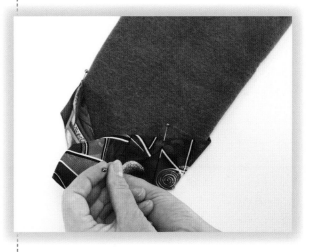

2 Overlap the tie ends on the front of the sleeve. Topstitch the sleeve trim in place, stopping just before the overlap.

3 Sew a blue button at the overlap on each sleeve.

Sew the Neck Trim

1 Sew the tie neck trim pieces together.

2 Measure 8" (20cm) from the ends of the sewn tie neck trim piece, gather tightly with thread at this point and secure.

3 Pin the tie trim ¼" (6mm) over the stitch line at the neck. Gather slightly to fit as you pin.

4 Hand-stitch in place through the back of the tie only.

Sew the Fabric Roses

1 See *Making Fabric Roses* (right) for directions, then make 3 roses from the tie rose pieces.

2 Using the photo above as a reference for positioning, sew the 3 roses to the center of the neck trim gather.

More on Fabric Roses

· Often these roses are made from ribbon, but they also can be created easily from fleece, felt or silk ties.

· Roses change in size depending on the length and width of the fabric strip. You can achieve varied effects by using strips cut from different sections of the same patterned fabric.

· To create a rosebud instead of a full bloom, don't wrap the fabric; instead, simply roll the strip toward you like a jelly roll.

MAKING FABRIC ROSES

1 Cut a 10–12" (25–30cm) strip from a tie. Fold 1 end down over the strip at a right angle.

2 Holding the folded end of the strip, roll the fabric toward you, wrapping the fabric clockwise with each roll. Keep the bottom even.

3 Continue until the full length of the strip is rolled and wrapped. Stitch through the bottom of the rolled fabric to hold the rose together.

1 black sweatshirt

1 broomstick skirt

1⅓ yds. (122cm) coordinating fabric

4 rhinestone buttons

Cutting mat

Iron and board

Large ruler

Matching thread

Needle

Pins

Quilt pencil or chalk (white)

Rotary cutter

Scissors

Sewing machine

Gypsy Girl Coat

Since broomstick skirts have colorful patchwork designs, the "fabric piecing" is already done for you, plus the fabrics are lightweight with a nice drape. One of these skirts, with its generous amount of fabric, lends itself to being transformed easily into an eye-catching, elegant coat with fabulous sleeves and collar accents.

Finished length: 40" (102cm).

Fit and Style

I love New Mexico and picked up three broomstick skirts while there. I wore the skirts some, but as my waistline expanded with age I looked like a sausage tied in the middle. Wanting to wear the skirts in a different way gave me the idea to refashion them into a long coat. It's my favorite, a flattering garment with a soft feminine feel.

When checking out thrift shops or your own closet, look for outdated pieces with lots of fabric to restyle.

Gypsy Girl
Sweatshirt L
Feminine and frilly
Ideal for a tall frame

Cut open
Cut
3"
5"
Cut
3"
Cut
5"
Cut
Cut open side seams
Stitching
Cut off bottom band

Inspiration Board for *Gypsy Girl Coat*
See the size and measurement guide on page 8 and compare the measurements of the sweatshirt you're using.

Back View of
Gypsy Girl Coat

PATTERNS TO BE PRINTED FROM CD:

Collar pieces 1 and 2 (Sheets #0-C01 and #0-C02)

CUTTING PLAN

Cut the waistband from the broomstick skirt.

Cut one 8" (20cm) length from the upper edge of the broomstick skirt.

Cut two 3" × 21" (8cm × 53cm) sleeve trim pieces from the 8" (20cm) length of broomstick fabric.

Cut 1 upper collar piece from the 8" (20cm) length of broomstick fabric.

Cut two 20" × 34" (51cm × 86cm) sleeve pieces from coordinating fabric.

Cut two 4" × 41" (10cm ×104cm) front trim pieces from coordinating fabric.

Cut two 4" × 21" (10cm × 53cm) belt pieces from coordinating fabric.

Cut 2 under collar pieces from cutoff sweatshirt fabric.

Cut one 23" (58cm) piece from the discarded bottom band of the sweatshirt.

See Sweatshirt Cutting Basics on pages 13–14.

Cut the Sweatshirt

1 Refer to the *Inspiration Board* on page 100 for the project cutting diagram. Measure 3" (8cm) down along the underarm seams of the sweatshirt sleeves and cut the sleeves off at this line.

2 Measure 5" (13cm) down from the underarm seams and cut the sweatshirt off at this line. Cut the sweatshirt open along the side seams.

3 Measure to find the center front of the sweatshirt and cut open.

4 Carefully cut off the bottom band with the stitching line intact. Cut a 23" (58cm) piece from this discarded band.

5 Cut the under collar pieces from the discarded sweatshirt piece.

Sew the Shoulder Pleats

1 Lay the sweatshirt flat, wrong side up.

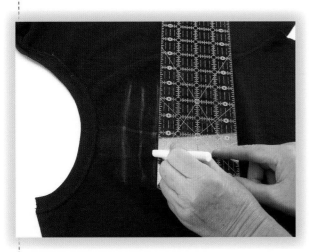

2 Beginning at the shoulder seam, measure 2" (5cm) in and mark. Repeat twice more.

3 Measure 3" (8cm) on either side of the shoulder seam, extending the 3 marks to 6" (15cm) in total pleat length. Repeat for the other shoulder.

4 Press along the drawn pleat lines and sew ¼" (6mm) on 1 side of each pleat line.

5 Press the pleats in 1 direction toward the shoulder.

Sew the Sleeves

1 Fold the broomstick sleeve trim pieces in half with wrong sides together and press.

2 Align and pin the trim pieces to the lower sleeve ends. Sew, finish and press the trim on each sleeve.

Sew the Front Trim

1 Fold all sides of the front trim pieces under ½" (13mm) and press, then press the trim pieces in half lengthwise.

2 Align the front trim pieces at the neck. Fold the trim pieces over the raw front edges and pin. Topstitch into place and press.

3 Sew 2 rows of gathering stitches ¼" (6mm) apart along each upper sleeve. Pull the stitches to fit the sweatshirt sleeve.

4 Pin each sleeve with right sides together. Sew and press.

5 Align the sleeves to the underarms of the sweatshirt and pin. Sew, finish the seams and press.

Sew the Skirt

1 Cut the skirt open along the seam. Trim to straighten the upper and side skirt edges.

2 Sew 2 rows of gathering stitches ¼" (6mm) apart along the upper skirt edge.

3 Pull the stitches to fit the skirt to the sweatshirt bodice and pin, aligning the front edges. Sew, finish the seams and press.

Sew the Collar

1 Sew the 2 under collar pieces together.

2 Match the sewn under collar piece with the upper collar piece, right sides together. Sew on all sides leaving a small center opening as shown on the pattern.

3 Clip the curves and corners, turn the collar and press.

4 Pin the collar to the top edge of the neckband with the right side of the collar against the inside edge of the neckband. The collar will stand up nicely when flipped to the outside.

5 Sew the collar into place.

Sew the Belt and Front Trim Buttons

1 Fold the belt pieces in half with right sides together. Sew each on 3 sides leaving the short end open. Turn and press.

2 Turn the sweatshirt bottom band piece inside out so the seam is on the inside.

3 Pin 1 band end to each open end of a belt piece. Sew, finish the seams and press.

4 Sew 4" (10cm) belt loops with black thread on both side seams of the coat.

5 Sew the rhinestone buttons to the front trim staggered 1" (25mm) apart on each trim edge.

YOU WILL NEED

1 cream sweatshirt

¼ yd. (23cm) Fabric A
(small rose floral)

¼ yd. (23cm) Fabric B
(green diagonal)

¼ yd. (23cm) Fabric C
(green circle)

⅓ yd. (30cm) Fabric D
(large pink floral)

¼ yd. (23cm) Fabric E
(large pink and green floral)

Five 1" (25mm) buttons

1 snap

½ yd. (46cm) braid trim

3 yds. (2.7m) bead fringe trim

Cutting mat

Embroidery needle

Iron and board

Large ruler

Matching thread

Pins

Quilt pencil or
chalk (white)

Rotary cutter

Scissors

Sewing
machine

Quilted Luxury Jacket

Perhaps you have a sweatshirt that you received as a gift—but it's an unattractive color or style or it's decorated with a design you'd rather not be seen wearing. Or perhaps your favorite sweatshirt has a dated style, a worn, faded design and a fit that's no longer flattering.

Here's the perfect solution! Revamp those sweatshirts with some leftover fabric pieces and beautiful trim. This luxurious quilted beauty will find a new place of honor in your closet.

Finished length: 22" (56cm).

Fit and Style

The sweatshirt used for this project originally sported floating ducks. I have nothing against ducks, I just don't like them swimming across my chest.

This technique covers up a has-been design and, depending on the choice of fabrics, makes a dramatic jacket.

Inspiration Board for *Quilted Luxury Jacket*

See the size and measurement guide on page 8 and compare the measurements of the sweatshirt you're using.

Back View of
Quilted Luxury Jacket

PATTERNS TO BE PRINTED FROM CD:

None

CUTTING PLAN

Cut one 3" × 22" (8cm × 56cm) Fabric A front trim piece.

Cut three 3¼" × 6" (8cm × 15cm) Fabric A small prairie point pieces.

Cut one 3" × 22" (8cm × 56cm) Fabric B front trim piece.

Cut three 3¼" × 6" (8cm × 15cm) Fabric B small prairie point pieces.

Cut three 6¼" × 12" (16cm × 30cm) Fabric B large prairie point pieces.

Cut one 5" × 22" (13cm × 56cm) Fabric C front trim piece.

Cut two 6" × 25" (15cm × 63cm) Fabric D lower band pieces.

Cut three 6¼" × 12" (16cm × 30cm) Fabric D large prairie point pieces.

Cut seven 6" (15cm) Fabric E square prairie point pieces.

Cut one 20" (51cm) neck piece from bead trim.

Cut one 48" (122cm) band piece from bead trim.

Cut two 14" (35cm) sleeve pieces from bead trim.

Cut three 4" (10cm) pieces from braid trim.

Cut the Sweatshirt

1 Refer to the *Inspiration Board* on page 105 for the project cutting diagram. Cut the cuffs and bottom band from the sweatshirt, leaving the neckband.

2 Cut the sweatshirt open along the side seams.

3 Measure 3" (8cm) up from the end of each sleeve and cut the sleeves off at this point.

4 Fold the sweatshirt in half, press and cut open along the center front line.

2 Press each square in half on the diagonal, then press again on the diagonal to create 3 large prairie points (1 goes on the back of the jacket). Trim any uneven raw edges.

3 Repeat steps 1–2 with the Fabric A and Fabric B small prairie point pieces to make 3 small prairie points.

4 Press the 7 squares cut from Fabric E into prairie points (see step 2). Trim any uneven raw edges.

About Prairie Points

A prairie point is a square of fabric pressed and folded into a triangle. Prairie points can be used in several ways as a decorative detail. Two or more fabrics can also be sewn together to create a prairie point, as in this project.

It can be easier to sew prairie points together first before affixing them to the sleeve or neckline. Position the prairie points on the garment, pinning them together. Remove the pinned prairie points carefully and sew to join, taking out the pins as you go.

Position the joined prairie points on the garment as before using only a couple of pins. This will keep the prairie points from moving or being folded over while they're stitched to the garment.

Finish the Sleeves

1 Alternate and overlap 3 small prairie points on the right side of each sleeve ¼" (6mm) from the edge. (For a narrower sleeve, only 2 prairie points may be needed for each.)

2 Pin, then sew the prairie points into place on each sleeve.

3 Pin bead trim over the raw edges of the prairie points and sew into place by hand or machine.

Sew the Prairie Points

1 Sew 1 Fabric B large prairie point piece to 1 Fabric D large prairie point piece to create a square with a ¼" (6mm) seam. Repeat twice more.

Sew the Front of Sweatshirt

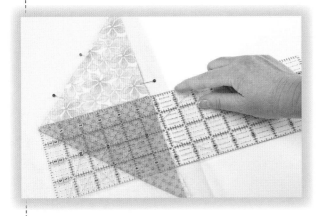

1 Pin 1 large prairie point 7" (18cm) in from each front edge of the sweatshirt. Match up the points.

2 Pin 1 small prairie point to the center of each large prairie point. Topstitch both large and small prairie points into place.

5 Align the top edge of the Fabric B front trim piece with the top of the Fabric A right front trim piece. Insert the raw edges of both the Fabric A trim piece and the sweatshirt into the Fabric B trim piece. Pin the Fabric B front trim piece in place, topstitch and press.

6 Fold both long sides of the Fabric C front trim piece ½" (13mm) under, then fold in half lengthwise and press.

7 Align the top edge of the Fabric C front trim piece with the left top edge of the sweatshirt. Insert the raw front edge of the sweatshirt into the Fabric C trim piece; the front trim piece should also cover the raw edges of the large and small prairie points.

8 Pin the Fabric C front trim piece into place, topstitch and press.

3 Press 1 long side of the Fabric A front trim piece ½" (13mm) under. Pin the pressed side of this trim piece over the raw edge of the prairie points on the right front side of the jacket. Topstitch into place.

4 Fold either long side of the Fabric B piece ½" (13mm) under, then fold in half lengthwise and press.

Sew the Side Seams

1 Align the side seams with right sides of the
sweatshirt together.

2 Sew, finish the seams and press.

Sew the Lower Band

1 Fold each lower band in half, right sides together,
and press.

2 Sew the short ends of the bands together. Turn
and press.

3 Pin the sewn lower band to the bottom edge of
sweatshirt with right sides together. Sew, finish the
seam and press.

4 Hand- or machine-sew the braided trim ¼" (6mm)
from the seam line.

Finish the Jacket

1 Hand- or machine-sew the beaded trim to the
neck edge.

2 Cut the braid trim into 3 equal lengths and form each
into a loop.

3 Sew the loops 4" (10cm) apart along the seam edge of
the right front trim. Align buttons with the loops on
the left side of the jacket and sew into place.

4 Press 1 point of a Fabric E prairie point under
½" (13mm) as shown in the photo on page 104 (see
the prairie point with the button at the neck edge). Pin
the raw edge of the prairie point at the right neck edge
over the seam line of the Fabric B front trim piece. (The
pressed-down point should be at the top.)

5 Sew the prairie point into place, then fold the point over and press toward the left side of the jacket.

6 Sew a snap top to the wrong side of the prairie point and a button to the right side (see the photo on page 104 for button positioning).

7 Line up the right and left front neck edges. Position and sew a snap bottom to the right side of the left front neck edge.

Finish the Back of Jacket

1 Pin the remaining Fabric E prairie point to the center of the remaining large prairie point, matching up the points. Topstitch the Fabric E prairie point into place (see the photo on page 105 for positioning).

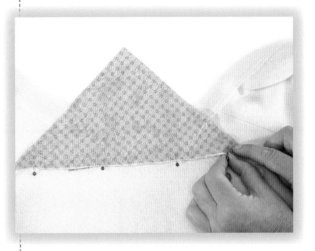

2 Pin the large prairie point, centered and with the point up, ½" (13mm) below the neckband on the back of the jacket with right sides of the jacket and prairie point facing.

3 Sew with a ¼" (6mm) seam. Flip the point down and press. Sew a button to the end of the point to hold it in place.

aaah, spa treats

At the end of a busy day or on a lazy Sunday morning, nothing is cozier than a robe to curl up in. Soft flannels and fleece equal inviting luxury.

Sweatshirt fleece is warm and comforting; paired with the soft fabrics in this chapter's projects, it creates a sumptuous treat for pampering yourself. (These designs also make lovely gifts.)

The three project styles are very different and suitable for any age. I made the delicate *Vintage Comfort Jacket* with my mom in mind, something she can to slip over her best nightie when she's curled up in bed, reading and resting. Delicate lace appliqués, an elegant detail, are easy to affix with fabric glue. The pretty gore insert allows ease of movement.

The *Sassy Chick Cover-Up* is something fun to slip on while painting your toenails—or painting the town, so to speak.

The *Ocean Dreams Hooded Robe* is ideal for a young woman off to college or moving into her first place. The popular and easy rail fence quilt pattern in soft blue flannels is fresh and soothing.

Whether it's a sassy slip-on gown or a dreamy ocean-themed robe, make a treat for yourself or a gift for that special someone!

YOU WILL NEED

1 green sweatshirt

½ yd. (46cm) eyelet fabric

Fabric glue

2½ yds. (2.3m) ⅜"-wide (9mm) white ribbon

1¼ yds. (144cm) ⅜"-wide (9mm) white beaded trim

½ yd. (46cm) 3"-wide (8cm) white lace

One 4" (10cm) lace appliqué with pearls

Cutting Mat

Iron and board

Large ruler

Matching and contrasting thread

Pins

Quilt pencil or chalk (white)

Rotary cutter

Scissors

Sewing machine

Vintage Comfort Jacket

Often a fabric will inspire a design. While browsing the aisles of my favorite fabric store, I came across this dyed shimmer eyelet fabric. Gorgeous lace trim and appliqué add beautiful detailing. This delicate bed jacket with lacy inserts is charming and makes a lovely gift for a special occasion like Mother's Day.

Finished length: 18" (46cm).

Fit and Style

My mom, like many others, has always saved her best nightie for the hospital. She also likes to have her arms covered to stay warm. This bed jacket is perfect for being comfortable in bed while covering the best nightie in proper style. For a day jacket, create in dramatic black and white with a large button closure instead of ribbon ties.

Vintage Comfort

Sweatshirt S

Gore inserts add style and extra width

Cut open

Cut open side seams

Cut off cuffs

Cut off bottom band

Cut off cuffs

Cut off cuffs

Inspiration Board for *Vintage Comfort Jacket*

See the size and measurement guide on page 8 and compare the measurements of the sweatshirt you're using.

Back View of
Vintage Comfort Jacket

PATTERNS TO BE PRINTED FROM CD:

Gore insert (Sheet #6-A01)

CUTTING PLAN

Cut 2 gore pieces from eyelet.

Cut one 4" × 44" (10cm × 112cm) collar ruffle from eyelet.

Cut the Sweatshirt

1 Refer to the *Inspiration Board* on page 113 for the project cutting diagram. Cut the bottom band and cuffs from the sweatshirt.

2 Cut open the sweatshirt along the side seams.

3 Fold the sweatshirt in half, press and cut open the front center line.

Sew the Collar Ruffle

1 Fold the ruffle piece in half lengthwise with right sides together; sew both ends closed.

2 Clip the corners. Turn the collar ruffle right side out and press.

3 Sew 2 rows of gathering stitches ⅛" (3mm) apart along the raw edge of the ruffle piece; pull the stitches to fit the neck.

4 Press the front edge of the sweatshirt ¾" (19mm) to the right side of the shirt.

TIP: Pressing the hem to the right side of the sweatshirt makes the fleece edge soft against the skin—especially nice in this bed jacket.

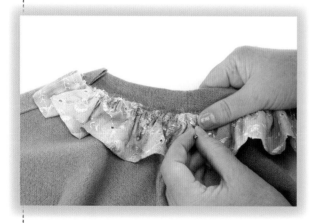

5 Pin the ruffle from the front folded edge of the sweatshirt along the seam line of the neckband.

6 Press the neckband in half over the raw edge of the ruffle and topstitch the neckband.

Sew the Sleeve Cuffs

1 Measure the sleeve length required for a correct fit.

2 Press a ¾" (19mm) hem to the right side of each sleeve.

3 Cut 2 lace pieces to fit the sleeve. Pin each lace piece ⅛" (3mm) above the sleeve hemlines.

4 Topstitch ¼" (6mm) from the top of the lace on each sleeve.

5 Topstitch ¼" (6mm) from the bottom edge of each sleeve.

Sew the Front Trim

1 Measure the sweatshirt front from under the collar ruffle to the unhemmed bottom. Cut 2 lengths of ribbon to this measurement.

2 Place 1 length of ribbon along each sweatshirt front. Topstitch into place along both edges of each ribbon.

Sew the Gore Inserts

1 Align 1 gore with the bottom edge of a front side seam, right sides together, and pin.

2 Sew the gore, press and trim the seam.

3 Repeat for the second gore on the opposite front side seam.

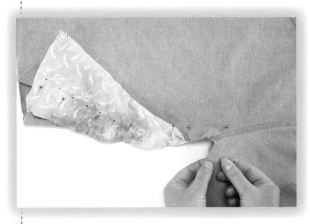

4 Align the front and back jacket side seams, right sides together, and pin.

5 Sew along the second side of each gore, finish the seams and press.

Finish the Bed Jacket

1 Press ¼" (6mm) of the bottom edge of the jacket under, then press another ¾" (19mm) under and topstitch.

2 Cut two 24" (61cm) lengths of ribbon.

3 Insert the end of 1 ribbon ½" (13mm) into the opening of the folded collar ruffle and hand-stitch into place. Repeat for the second ribbon.

4 Measure and cut 2 lengths of pearl trim to fit the front edges of the jacket from under the collar to the hem.

5 Center and glue each piece of pearl trim over the white ribbon trim sewn to each front edge of the jacket.

6 Cut and sew or glue 2 small pearl trim pieces over the folded collar.

7 Pin the pearl appliqué piece to the upper left front of the jacket. Sew into place or adhere with fabric glue.

YOU WILL NEED

1 black sweatshirt

1¼ yds. (114cm) print fabric*

4 yds. (3.6m) 3"-wide (8cm) black lace

1¼ yds. (114cm) ¾"-wide (19mm) black elastic sequin trim

2" (5cm) bead cluster

Fabric glitter

Fabric glue

Cutting mat

Iron and board

Large ruler

Matching thread

Needle

Pins

Quilt pencil or chalk (white)

Rotary cutter

Scissors

Sewing machine

Stylus or ballpoint pen

Transfer paper (white or light-colored)

I used Scrollie by Loralie Designs™ for this project.

Sassy Chick Cover-Up

This vivacious ruffled dress-style cover-up projects a little sass thanks to fabric from a very fun collection. The glitter embellishments and flirty black lace are for those special spa moments when you might have an audience. Just add a feather boa, high heel slippers and cha-cha-cha!

Finished length: 40" (102cm).

Fit and Style

An attractive scoop neck and dropped waist make for a comfortable, easy-to-slip-on wearable. Ruffles and lace give a flirty feminine feel to this cover-up.

Inspiration Board for *Sassy Chick Cover-Up*
See the size and measurement guide on page 8 and compare the measurements of the sweatshirt you're using.

Back View of
Sassy Chick Cover-Up

PATTERNS TO BE PRINTED FROM CD:

Scroll design template (Sheet #6-B01)

CUTTING PLAN

Cut two 18" × 44" (46cm × 112cm) lower pieces from print fabric.
Cut two 4" × 44" (10cm × 112cm) sleeve pieces from print fabric.

Cut the Sweatshirt

1 Refer to the *Inspiration Board* on page 117 for the project cutting diagram. Cut the neckband, bottom band and cuffs from the sweatshirt.

2 Cut the sweatshirt open along the side seams.

3 Lay the sweatshirt flat right side down. Place a ruler across the full width of 1 sleeve ½" (13mm) from the seam line.

4 Draw a line across the sleeve and cut. Repeat for the second sleeve.

5 With the sweatshirt flat, mark 1" (25mm) from the neck every 2" (5cm).

6 Draw to join the marks and cut along this line.

Sew the Sleeve Ruffles

1 Fold each ruffle piece in half lengthwise, right sides together, and sew the ends closed. Clip the corners on each ruffle piece, turn and press.

2 Sew 2 rows of gathering stitches ⅛" (3mm) apart along the raw edge of each ruffle piece. Pull the stitches to fit and pin each ruffle along a sleeve edge. Sew each ruffle into place, finish the seams and press.

Finish the Neckline

1 Press ½" (13mm) along the neckline to the right side of the sweatshirt. Use fabric glue to fix the hem into place.

2 Starting at the shoulder, glue the black elastic sequin trim along the neck edge.

Make the Scroll Design

1 Print the scroll design from the CD (Sheet #6-B01) onto regular paper.

2 Lay the sweatshirt flat, right side up. Using the photo on page 119 as a reference, position the paper with the scroll design ½" (13mm) from the bottom and side of the sweatshirt. Pin the paper at the top.

3 Slip a sheet of white or light-colored transfer paper under the scroll design; make sure the transfer side of the paper is facing down. Trace the lines of the scroll design with a stylus or ballpoint pen. Be careful not to pierce the transfer paper. Slide up the scroll design sheet so that the end of the scroll design meets the top of the first transferred scroll. Repeat the transfer.

Sew the Bottom

1 Align both bottom fabric pieces with right sides together. Sew 1 side seam, finish and press.

2 Along the bottom of the sewn fabric pieces, press ¼" (6mm) under, then another ½" (13mm) under and topstitch.

3 Sew 2 rows of gathering stitches ¼" (6mm) apart along the top of the fabric piece.

4 Carefully draw a thin line of glue along the scroll design, beginning at the bottom and working in 3" (8cm) sections.

5 Sprinkle glitter generously over the glued portion of the scroll. Continue gluing and sprinkling glitter.

6 Let the glue and glitter dry thoroughly. Shake off the excess glitter.

Glittering Success

After you apply glue to a new section of the scroll, carefully lift the sweatshirt from the bottom edge and shake the glitter forward along the fresh glue line. Add more glitter as needed.

Sew the Side Seams

1 Align the side seams with right sides together.

2 Sew, then finish the seams.

4 Sew 1 row of gathering stitches on the lace piece 1" (25mm) from the top. Pull the stitches to fit the lace and pin to the right side of the fabric piece hemline with stitches aligned. Topstitch the lace into place.

5 Sew the second side seam of the fabric bottom piece with right sides together.

Finish the Cover-Up

1 With right sides together, match the side seams. Pin the bottom fabric piece to the sweatshirt along the edge at the center back, front and side seams.

2 Pull the gathering stitches on the bottom fabric piece to fit the top, adding more pins.

3 Sew the bottom fabric piece and the top together, then repeat the seam for added strength. Finish the seam and press.

4 Sew or pin the bead cluster to the center front neckline.

YOU WILL NEED

1 white sweatshirt

1½ yds. (1.3m) coordinating Fabric A

1½ yds. (1.3m) coordinating Fabric B

1½ yds. (1.3m) white flannel

1½ yds. (1.3m) white ribbon

1 skein embroidery floss or
1 ball pearl cotton in blue

1 package 5mm pearl beads

5 pearl buttons

6" (15cm) embroidery hoop

Cutting mat

Embroidery needle

Iron and board

Large ruler

Masking or art tape

Matching thread

Pins

Quilt pencil or chalk (white)

Rotary cutter

Sewing machine

Scissors

Stylus or ballpoint pen

Transfer paper or
dressmaker's
carbon (colored)

Ocean Dreams Hooded Robe

I grew up by the ocean. One of the happiest summers of my mom's life was when she was pregnant with me and spent the whole summer at a seaside cottage. During the day she played on the beach with friends, and after work my dad would join her. Every year we all get together for a week at the cottage by the ocean. This dreamy robe is inspired by those lovely salt-kissed days.

The easy and popular rail fence quilt pattern finishes off this hooded haven of a robe. The whimsical shell embroidery is reminiscent of traditional redwork.

Finished length: 40" (102cm).

Fit and Style

I chose the flannel collection for this robe for its soothing patterns and softness. Blue and white are a classic combination to pair with a pristine white sweatshirt.

Inspiration Board for *Ocean Dreams Hooded Robe*
See the size and measurement guide on page 8 and compare the measurements of the sweatshirt you're using.

Back View of
Ocean Dreams Hooded Robe

PATTERNS TO BE PRINTED FROM CD:

Shell embroidery designs templates (Sheet #6-C01)

Hood pieces 1 and 2 (Sheets #6-C02 and #6-C03)

Pocket (Sheet #6-C04)

CUTTING PLAN

Cut eleven 3" × 42" (8cm × 107cm) strips from Fabric A.

Cut eleven 3" × 42" (8cm × 107cm) strips from Fabric B.

Cut one 6" × 12" (15cm × 30cm) cuff piece from Fabric A.

Cut one 6" × 12" (15cm × 30cm) cuff piece from Fabric B.

Cut one 3" × 13" (8cm × 33cm) front trim piece from Fabric A.

Cut one 3" × 13" (8cm × 33cm) front trim piece from Fabric B.

Cut 2 hood pieces from Fabric A.

Cut 2 hood lining pieces from Fabric B.

Cut two 28" × 30" (71cm × 76cm) lining pieces from white flannel.

Cut 2 pockets from sweatshirt remnant.

Cut the Sweatshirt

1 Refer to the *Inspiration Board* on page 121 for the project cutting diagram. Cut the neckband and cuffs from the sweatshirt.

2 Measure 5" (13cm) down from the underarm seams and cut the sweatshirt along this line.

3 Measure to find the center front of the sweatshirt and cut open along this line.

4 Cut 2 pockets on the fold from the cutoff sweatshirt piece.

Embroider the Shell Designs

1 Print the shell design from the CD (Sheet #6-C01) onto regular paper. Using the photo on page 120 as a reference, position the paper with the shell design on the right side of the sweatshirt. Pin the paper at the top.

2 Slip a sheet of colored transfer paper or dressmaker's carbon under the shell design; make sure the transfer side of the paper is facing down. Trace the lines of the scroll design with a stylus or ballpoint pen. Be careful not to pierce the transfer paper.

3 Insert the section of fabric with the shell design into an embroidery hoop. Make sure the fabric is taut.

4 With blue floss or pearl cotton, backstitch the outline and inner lines of the shell. (See *Adding Embroidery* on page 15.)

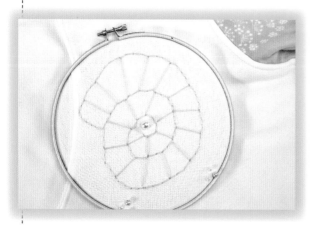

5 Sew pearl beads in groups of 3 as shown in the photo above. Sew a pearl button to the center of the shell.

She Sews Seashells…

Embroider a different shell design from Sheet #6-C01 from the CD, or transfer and work a couple more shells on the front of the robe.

Sew the Cuffs

1 Fold the Fabric A and Fabric B cuff pieces in half and sew each on 3 sides, leaving a 2" (5cm) opening to turn. Turn each cuff piece and press.

2 Pin each cuff to a sleeve end, overlapping the sleeve edge ½" (13mm).

3 Topstitch the cuffs into place and overlap the ends. Sew a pearl button at each overlapped sleeve end.

Sew the Hood

1 Sew the Fabric A hood pieces together. Repeat with the Fabric B hood lining pieces. Clip the curves.

2 Align the Fabric A and B hood pieces with right sides together. Sew, leaving a 3" (8cm) opening to turn as indicated on the pattern.

3 Clip the curves and corners. Turn the hood and press.

4 Pin the hood to the lower edge of the neck, in ½" (13mm) from the front edge, with right sides together.

5 Gather any excess sweatshirt fabric at the neck evenly between the shoulder seams. Sew the hood into place.

Sew the Front Trim

1 Fold in ½" (13mm) on 3 sides of the Fabric A and Fabric B front trim pieces and press.

2 Fold each front trim piece in half lengthwise and press.

3 With the folded edge at the top, pin the Fabric A front trim piece over the front edge of the side of the robe with the Fabric B cuff. Repeat, pinning the Fabric B front trim piece on the side with the Fabric A cuff.

4 Starting at the bottom, topstitch 1 trim piece into place, then continue to topstitch along the front of the hood and around to and down the opposite front trim.

Sew the Lower Robe

1 Sew pairs of Fabric A and Fabric B strips together, making 11 strip sets.

2 Mark the ruler with masking or art tape at 5½" (14cm). Measure and cut each strip set into seven 5½" (14cm) blocks.

3 Lay out 12 blocks into 2 rows as shown in the diagram below. Sew each row of blocks.

4 Press each seam allowance toward the darker Fabric A.

5 Pin row sets together carefully. Sew blocks into six 2-row strips. Without steam, press the seams away from the cross seam to avoid distorting the fabric.

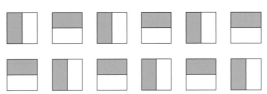

Pattern for Blocks Sewn into Rows

6 Sew the lining pieces together. Press and finish the seams.

7 Align the front of the lower robe with the lining and pin. Sew completely around all 4 sides, leaving a 6" (15cm) opening at the center top for turning. Trim the corners, turn the lower robe and press.

8 Pin the lower robe to the sweatshirt bodice and sew. Topstitch the seam as well as the lower robe front edges.

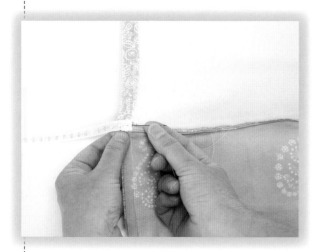

9 Cut the white ribbon in half and fold over ¼" (6mm) of 1 end of each ribbon. Sew the folded ends of the ribbons to the left and right inside front at the bodice/lower robe seam.

Sew the Shell Pockets

1 Fold the pocket pieces with the fleece as the right side.

2 Sew 3 sides, leaving an opening between notches for turning. Turn the pockets and press.

3 Mark 4 equal diagonal lines on each pocket.

4 Embroider the diagonal lines with blue floss or pearl cotton using the running stitch. Sew a pearl button in the corner where the lines come together.

5 Pin each pocket with the edge 8" (20cm) down from the seam line and in 3" (8cm) from the front edge. Topstitch into place.

resources

Support your local craft and fabric retailers. If you are unable to find a particular product, contact the manufacturer to locate a store or mail-order source.

Beadalon
(866) 4BEADALON (423-2325)
www.beadalon.com
(beads)

Beacon Adhesives, Inc.
(914) 699-3405
www.beaconadhesives.com
(Fabri-tac™)

Berwick Offray LLC
(800) 327-0350
www.offray.com
(Offray satin and grosgrain ribbon)

Caron International
www.caron.com
(yarns)

Clover Needlecraft, Inc.
(800) 233-1703
www.clover-usa.com
(notions, mini iron)

Coats & Clark
(800) 648-1479
www.coatsandclark.com
(embroidery floss, pearl cotton, yarns, accessories)

The Electric Quilt Company
(419) 352-1134 or (800) 356-4219
www.electricquilt.com
(ink-jet fabric sheets)

Expo International, Inc.
(800) 542-4367 or (713) 782-6600
www.expointl.com
(beaded and specialty trims, wholesale only)

Fiskars Brands, Inc.
(866) 348-5661
www.fiskarscrafts.com
(scissors, rotary cutter, self-healing cutting mat, acrylic rulers)

Kandi Corp
(800) 985–2634
www.kandicorp.com
(hot-fix applicators, crystals and studs)

Kreinik Manufacturing Co., Inc.
(800) 537-2166
www.kreinik.com
(iron-on threads, metallic braid)

Loralie Designs™
(817) 573-5702
www.LoralieDesigns.com
(Scrollie, Cat Lady and other fun panel fabrics)

Therm O Web, Inc.
(800) 323-0799
www.thermoweb.com
(HeatnBond® iron-on adhesive)

Walnut Hollow
(800) 950-5101
www.walnuthollow.com
(Creative Textile Tool™)

metric conversion chart

TO CONVERT	TO	MULTIPLY BY
inches	centimeters	2.54
centimeters	inches	0.4
feet	centimeters	30.5
centimeters	feet	0.03
yards	meters	0.9
meters	yards	1.1

about the author

Author and designer Debra Quartermain combines her talent and her love of inspiring creativity in others by designing stylish wearables and home décor and by needle felting whimsical characters. Her designs have been featured in such magazines as *Bead Unique*, *Crafts 'n Things*, *Country Marketplace*, *Create and Decorate*, *Today's Creative Homearts* and *PaperCrafts*. Debra has authored four books, including *Nursery Decor*, *Easy-to-Sew Playful Toys* and *Sweatshirts: Figure, Fit, Fashion* (Krause Publications, an imprint of F+W Media, Inc.), and she's collaborated on several other titles. Debra works with manufacturers to produce designs and instructions for their products and has designed patterns for Butterick/McCalls. As a speaker, she offers an informative, entertaining presentation sharing her love of RE-creativity. A current member of the Craft and Hobby Association (CHA), Debra writes a regular column for *Today's Creative Homearts* called "Make It Green" as well as her popular blog "My Reclaimed Life."

Debra creates and lives in a colorful fabric-filled design studio in Fredericton, New Brunswick, Canada, with daughters, cats and good friends always nearby. Connect with Debra at MyCraftivity.com; view her portfolio at www.pqexpressions. com; and read her blogs at www.debraquartermain.typepad.com/confessionsofa stitchchick and www.debraquartermain.typepad.com/myreclaimedlife.

about the illustrator

Deborah Peyton is a well-known Canadian cartoonist and illustrator. Through her Fine-Tooning business, she has published books as well as a daily cartoon series that appears in several Canadian and U.S. newspapers. She has illusrated many textbooks and promotional materials and developed original characters for several projects. Humorous greeting cards and clever caricatures showcase her varied talents as well.

At present, much of her work consists of illustrating books, several of which are Krause publications: *Easy-to-Sew Playful Toys*, *Contemporary Machine-Embroidered Fashions* and *Sweatshirts: Figure, Fit Fashion*. Deborah is a member of the National Cartoonists Society.

She shares her home in the beautiful coastal city of Halifax, New Brunswick, Canada with her husband, two daughters, Peek-a-boo the rescued one-eyed cat and Curtis the dog. More about Deborah and her portfolio can be seen at www.pqexpressions.com.

index

More fun, fabulous sweatshirt transformations!

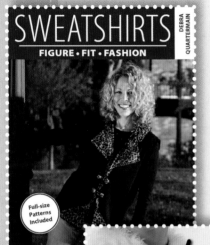

Sweatshirts
FIGURE ~ FIT ~ FASHION

Debra Quartermain

Fashion-forward sweatshirts are not only comfortable, they're stylish, too! Explore techniques for creating blazers, cardigans and tunics from sweatshirts. Illustrated with over 200 color photos.

Paperback, 128 pages, #Z0750.
ISBN-10: 0-89689-486-X   **ISBN-13: 978-0-89689-486-0**

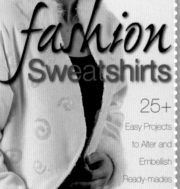

Fashion Sweatshirts
25+ EASY PROJECTS TO ALTER AND EMBELLISH READY-MADES

Lorine Mason

These 29 transformations of ready-made sweatshirts for women and children use sewing, embroidery, knitting and crocheting techniques as well as embellishments such as buttons, fringes and applique.

Paperback, 128 pages, #FSHSW.
ISBN-10: 0-87349-912-3   **ISBN-13: 978-0-87349-912-5**

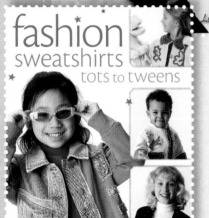

Fashion Sweatshirts Tots to Tweens

Lorine Mason

With this step-by-step guide, turn a simple, inexpensive sweatshirt into a personal design statement for kids to young teens in sizes 2T to 10–12. All 20 projects include printed patterns.

Paperback, 128 pages, #Z2405.
ISBN-10: 0-89689-704-4   **ISBN-13: 978-0-89689-704-5**